P9-EGB-263

BEYOND THE

STUMP FARM

YA 819.85.402 Adams

Adams, R.
Beyond the stump farm.
JUL 2 9 2008

PRICE: $18.95 (3559/he   )

OTHER BOOKS BY ROBERT J. ADAMS

*   *   *

THE STUMP FARM

HORSE COP

FISH COP

THE ELEPHANT'S TRUNK

THE SOUTH ROAD

SKUNKS & HOUND DOGS

IN THE SHADOW OF THE ROCKIES

DYNAMITE HILL

BEYOND THE

STUMP FARM

ROBERT J. ADAMS

MEGAMY

DEDICATION

To my parents Florence and Bob Adams.
To my grandparents Veona and John Ernst.
To all those Canadians who struggled and persevered to eke
out an existence from an unforgiving land during the dirty
thirties and the war years.

DISCLAIMER

The stories you are about to read are all true. The men, women
and children you will read about are all people from my past.
I have take the liberty of changing their names to protect their
identities. Although I view the past as very humorous they may
not.

Copyright © by Robert J. Adams and Kelly Hymanyk
First Printed in 1997
2ND Printing in 1998
3RD Printing in 1999
4th Printing in 2002
5th Printing in 2005
Printed in Canada

All Rights Reserved. No part of this work covered by the copyright hereon may be reproduced in any form or by any means--graphic, electronic or mechanical--without prior written permission of the publisher or a licence from The Canadian Copyright Licensing Agency(Access Copyright), except for reviewers who may quote brief passages. For an Access Copyright licence, visit www.accesscopyright.ca or call toll free to 1-800-893-5777.

THE PUBLISHER:
Megamy Publishing Ltd.
P. O. Box 3507
Spruce Grove, Alberta, Canada T7X 3A7
E-mail: megamy@compusmart.ab.ca

Canadian Cataloguing in Publication Data
Adams, Robert J., 1938-
    Beyond the stump farm

ISBN 0-9681916-2-2

1. Adams Robert J., 1938- --Anecdotes. 2. Farm Life--Alberta--Anecdotes. 3. Canadian wit and humor
(English)* I. Title.
PS8551.D3224B49 1997   C818'.5402   C97-910850-0
PR9199.3.A28B49 1997

Senior Editor: Kelly Hymanyk
Copy Editor: Linda Caldwell
Design, Layout and Production: Kelly Hymanyk
Cover: Guideline Graphics
Printing: Quebecor World

CONTENTS

ACKNOWLEDGEMENTS

I would like to thank my family for all the encouragement and the selfless giving of their time and efforts. To my wife Martha for putting up with my demands, not to mention the havoc I created, in my quest to complete the manuscript. To Kelly, my daughter, my editor, my harshest critic, the love of my life for taking on the unenviable task of meeting me face to face over each and every word. To Bill for keeping a low profile and calming troubled waters.

To my brother and sisters, Larry Adams, Gwen Macara and Judy Thomson for late night visits reminiscing about the stump farm, refreshing old memories and collectively putting the past back together.

To the Forest Rangers of the 1950's, tough hardy individuals accustomed to the rigours of a life out-of-doors. They were the role models that helped mould the character of a young Bob Adams.

To the Alberta Forest Service for taking a chance and giving me, a farm boy, a summer job during lean times when jobs were scarce.

INTRODUCTION

It is said that laughter is the best medicine. This could be why readers everywhere have embraced the writings of Robert J. Adams. Simply put, Adams' stories make us feel good when we read them. Young or old, we laugh and remember as he spins his boyhood tales.

Beyond the Stump Farm picks up where *The Stump Farm* left off and we continue to share the adventures of Bobby, a young boy entering the often misunderstood years of adolescence. His innocent charm compels us to read on and revisit our own years of innocence long forgotten.

MEGAMY PUBLISHING

BEYOND THE

STUMP FARM

THE OLYMPIC WANNABE

I spent days pulling bucket after bucket of water from the depths of the earth, flooding a small patch of ground between the well and the barn. It was not an ideal place, but it was the best and only place for a future Olympic skater to put his efforts into developing a rink. Especially an ice skating rink that was to be located on the stump farm.

Man, I was excited when I received my first pair of skates earlier in the year. They were a pair of beat-up old hand-me-downs that showed little proof of the black dye that had originally covered the leather. The boot was badly worn and carried many scars from years of battles with other skates, boards, rocks and who knew what. The toes had taken the brunt of the wear and tear. They were badly cut and large pieces of leather were either missing or hanging loosely over the sole. Not a single seam was intact. Loose threads protruded and on some seams gaps were beginning to show. The laces were a series of knots that held a conglomeration of lace, cord and twine together. How many other future Olympians or NHL hockey players had learned to skate in these very skates? I had no idea, but it mattered little, for I was on my way to greatness, as soon as I finished the rink, that is.

I thought back to the first time that I tried the skates on. I was sitting in the kitchen and I slipped my foot into them. No problem there, I have small feet and they were a couple of sizes too big, so naturally my foot dropped right into the bottom of the sole. I was having difficulty pulling some of the knots through the eyelets, so Mom helped me lace them up. "How do they feel?" she asked after laboriously working the knots through the holes.

"They feel good," I replied as I wriggled my foot around the inside of the boot. Actually, I think my foot was swimming around in there, trying to find one side of the boot or the other. With little success, I might add.

"Are they too big?" she inquired, giving me a questioning look. "They look like they're too big for you."

"No. They fit good," I answered as my feet swam another lap.

"Stand up and walk around," she ordered and stood back to observe.

I slipped off the chair and gently let the skates touch the linoleum. That felt pretty good, so I stood up and put my weight on the blades. The room moved, two ways at once, as one blade went north one south. My ankles hit the floor and instant pain shot up through my legs. My knees collapsed and I grabbed for the table. "Boy, I didn't know skates were so hard to stand on." I winced as both ankles had these little shooting pains darting through them. I tried to straighten my feet, but the skates wouldn't allow it.

"That's what I figured," Mom said with a sigh, "they're too big for you."

"No, Mom. They fit real good. Honest, they fit me. Please let me keep them," I pleaded, realizing that if they didn't fit I could very easily be losing my prized possessions.

"Take them off and we'll see what we can do to make them fit," Mom directed.

Reluctantly I unlaced the skates and they fell from my feet and dropped on the floor. Mom dug out an old Eaton's catalogue that she had been saving for the outdoor biffy and tore off several of the shiny pages. These she carefully folded before stuffing them into the bottom of one of the boots. I watched in amazement as she worked a miracle. Before long, with the aid of the catalogue, a pair of scissors and some country know-how, Mom had those skates fitting fairly snugly on my feet.

Once more, with the newly stuffed skates laced firmly to my feet, I slid from the chair and onto the floor. My ankles didn't realize that the skates now fit and they did a repeat performance. The skate blades shot to the sides and again I was standing on my ankles, desperately trying to get the skate blades underneath me.

"Your ankles are a little weak," Mom said. "But

they'll get stronger as you learn how to skate."

One thing the stump farm definitely lacked was a skating area. There was no lake or pond on which to skate. The nearest rink was in Edson and I had been fortunate enough to be able to get into town a few times where I could practice. There on the large indoor skating rink with its glassy smooth ice, I learned how to skate. And learn to skate, I did. My ankles got stronger. At least they no longer hurt as I battled my way around the boards.

The Edson arena was a huge building covered with corrugated metal siding and roofing. A tinny old building that held the cold inside like it was a deep freeze. It always seemed to be colder inside then it was outside. In fact, every time I skated in that arena, my feet would freeze. I would sit in the dressing room for the longest time, often with tears in my eyes, waiting for my toes to thaw out before walking home. It never ceased to amaze me, how my toes could freeze when they and half the Eaton's catalogue were bound tightly inside my skates and I was inside a building, to boot?

However, my skating abilities developed fairly well in the frigid old building, and I along with a number of other young skaters had been selected to skate in the Edson Ice Carnival. It was an exciting time. I would be performing in front of relatives and friends. I would be a star.

I was in a group of several budding stars whose routine was to skate around the rink in a predetermined rotation. We were to be stars in the Milky Way and what better way to show the audience that we represented the Milky Way then to carry milk bottles.

The bottles we were carrying were very large and cut out of cardboard. Each bottle was about two-and-a-half-feet high and about a foot wide. They were painted white to show the audience that they were actually full of milk.

After a couple of laps around the arena, showing the audience that we could indeed skate, each little star in the Milky Way would skate to the centre of the arena. There, after kneeling or most often falling down, the little star would stand the milk bottle on its side, while another little star would break from the line, skate forward and attempt to jump the bottle. The audience would cheer each time one of the little stars sailed over the bottle.

I couldn't wait for my turn. I could just hear everyone cheering as I leapt high, clearing the bottle and landing gracefully on the other side. When my turn finally arrived, I watched as another little star skated to the centre of the rink, stopped and stood the bottle on its side. I took off like a racer with long graceful strides. I was flying. I was no longer just one of the little stars, I was a shooting star, the picture of grace and beauty as I approached the obstacle.

I had already committed myself to the jump when I noticed it. I couldn't believe my eyes! The little star holding the bottle had his eyes closed. He was flinching and the bottle was moving towards me. I had a moving target. Holy cow, I thought, I have enough trouble hitting a standing target. Swerve out of the way, my head yelled at my feet. Too late, one foot was already in the air, my graceful leap had just taken an ugly turn. The large crowd oohed and aahed as my lead foot caught the moving bottle. I was suddenly flying through the air, my arms were flailing wildly. It was not a graceful performance. It was a disaster. I crashed into the little star, the one with closed eyes, the one who had good cause to flinch as I approached. Instantly two little stars skittered along the ice surface in a tangle of arms, legs, skates and cardboard milk bottles. Those in the crowd who were not oohing and aahing were laughing hysterically. I could hear the laughter like a deafening roar. That's the last time I'm going to skate in the Milky Way, I told myself.

Just my dumb luck to have someone who couldn't hold the bottle still, I thought as I quickly collected myself and raced back to my place in the line, leaving the other star laying on the ice. I watched as everyone else had their bottle held perfectly still. Although some stumbled, they each managed to clear the jump and each time the audience would roar their appreciation.

After their on-ice performance, the little stars of the Milky Way skated once more around the ice surface and then behind the large curtain at the end of the arena where the rest of the skaters were waiting to go on. The little stars got to stand around and watch the other skaters that went out to perform. I was peeking through cracks in the curtain watching to see what was happening on the ice.

I stared in amazement as several barrels were rolled out to the centre of the ice and a man flashed around the outside of the rink. He was really flying when he left the outside surface and cut down the centre of the arena. In one smooth motion he leapt over the barrels and easily landed on his feet on the far side. The audience roared their approval.

But it was the fancy figure skaters that caught my eye. The girls with their short skirts and mesh stockings who stood beside the little stars of the Milky Way before going out and dazzling the audience. I watched, fascinated with the way they could jump and spin and glide around on one leg. The audience would cheer and whistle as they finished their routine. Behind the curtain there would be big smiles, hugs and kisses. Everyone was so happy.

There was one skater, a girl from Edmonton, who skated all by herself. I heard someone say that she was going to skate in the Olympics. I decided right then and there that's what I wanted to do, too. "I want to skate in the Olympics," I told Mom after the carnival.

"That's good," she replied, "but it takes an awful lot of practice to get good enough and we don't have any ice close to the farm. It's a long way to walk to town every day."

I decided that I would practise every day, but first I needed ice that was closer to the farm. I could build a rink, I convinced myself. Yes, I could build a rink right on the stump farm.

The water trough for the animals was situated fairly close to the well. In fact, it was just on the other side of the pole fence. In the winter time water had to be drawn for the livestock and the closer the trough to the well, the less distance the water had to be packed.

It was here, close, very close to the water trough that I had decided to create a skating rink where a future Olympic skater could train on a daily basis. I marked out a small area close to the well and the trough and commenced to tramp down the snow. The higher snow around the edges would act as the boards.

When the snow had been tramped down I couldn't wait to get an ice surface on which to skate. I immediately started to draw water, one pail at a time. This was going to be a long drawn-out project, I concluded, as each bucket of water continued to disappear into the snow.

One of the cows had obviously heard me drawing water and must have figured it was time for a drink. That dumb cow, she ambled up from the barn and walked right through the centre of my rink. Her hoofs sank a good five inches in the wet snow. "Get off my rink, you stupid cow," I yelled and rushed to chase her off.

Now cows have never been too smart and this cow was no exception. She looked at me and raised her tail as if in defiance and promptly dropped about two gallons of pee. Right on the ice surface of the future Olympian. I was outraged at this insult. Then it suddenly struck me. Hey, I thought, this is unexpected, a gift from the gods. The cows and horses could also provide a little help. They had to walk close to the ice surface every day to get to the trough. Often, as they took on a little water, they would also pee a little. (Actually, it was more like pee a lot.) More liquid for my rink, albeit a different colour and not necessarily where I would have placed it, but then water was not all that abundant on the farm. Pee was after all water and I was about to take all the help I could get. I extended the size of the rink to be sure that I got all the cow and horse pee.

Building the rink was a tedious task. Water was poured over the surface one bucket at a time. There was also a little slop-over from the trough, but that just built rough ridges. The livestock co-operated and dropped a pee or two a day, but it took a long time to get a patch of ice large enough to skate on. I persisted and eventually, thanks to long cold winters, the day finally arrived when I figured there was enough ice.

I donned the skates. The beat-up hand-me-downs, the hockey skates that lacked the little teeth the figure skates had on the toes. I was ready to begin my Olympic quest.

"Hey Mom," I called, "do you want to come out and watch me figure skate on my rink?"

"I don't think you'll be able to figure skate out there," she cautioned. "That ice is pretty rough. You'll be lucky if you're even able to stand up without breaking your neck."

"It'll be fine," I chirped. "It's not as big as the arena, but it's pretty good, you'll see. I betcha that I'll be able to skate on one leg, too."

"Don't be too sure about that," Mom said, smiling at me as I laced up the skates and headed out the door.

Walking from the house to the home-made rink was pretty easy. The blades cut into the packed snow along the path. It was just like walking in shoes, I thought as I strode on.

As I passed the well, it was difficult to see where the little rink actually began. With water and livestock pee splashed around on the snow I found that every once in a while a skate would hit a patch of hidden ice. When this happened the skate would shoot out from under me, taking my leg with it. I made some pretty fancy pirouettes between the well and the rink as my body twisted and turned in an attempt to stay upright.

It was no use. There were just too many small patches of ice that had formed in the snow. Hidden from the eye, they created an insurmountable obstacle course. Covered with snow from several unexpected crashes, I crawled the last few feet to the ice surface. I looked back at the house. No one was watching. I was glad that Mom hadn't come outside to see that little display.

I struggled to my feet and prepared to take the first stride on my new rink. It was then that I realized the surface wasn't very big. In fact, skating on the little rink was nothing more then going in circles, very little circles. Three or four strides in any direction would take me from one side of the ice to the other. There would be no long graceful glides here. The future Olympian would have to be inventive or end up in the snow that formed the sideboards.

Pushing forward with one leg, the blade and my ankle skidded along the rough surface. I found that it was much easier to skate if I used my ankles as well as the blade to stand on. Anyway, my ankles didn't hurt anymore. I took another stride and I was sailing right along on the second skate when it stopped suddenly. I flew forward face-first on the ice and skidded into the snow on the other side. That hadn't been in the plan, I thought as I looked back to see why I had suddenly fallen.

There it was, sticking up through the ice. A cow pie frozen solid with only the tip of it protruding through the ice. I learned one thing for certain, my skates weren't going to be able to skate over or through a frozen cow pie. Not even a very small bit of a frozen cow pie. I looked around the ice surface. It was mottled with various shades of brown and yellow from the livestock contribution and I noticed that there were several cow pies that were partially buried in the ice. There was also an ample supply of road apples, the horses' donation to the cause. The future Olympian would have to learn to skate around these obstacles.

Undaunted, once again I struggled to my feet, this time watching for the brown lumps that indicated a hazard. I took another stride forward. I was doing fine skating with my head down watching for pies and apples when a skate suddenly dropped into a hole. Once more I took an unscheduled dive into the snow at the edge of the rink. This time the obstacle was a hoof print. The outline of the hoof of a cow was perfectly imbedded in the ice.

The pee was another problem. It built up on the ice surface wherever the animal happened to raise its tail. Although the skate blade would pass over this build-up it was rough enough to throw me off stride. The result would usually be another face-first trip to the snow bank.

I stormed back into the house. "I can't skate out there," I ranted. "Those stupid cows have ruined my ice. They've crapped and peed all over it. I can't even stand up without falling over a cow pie or into a hoof print."

"I guess you'll just have to keep the livestock off of your rink then," Mom replied.

"How am I going to do that?" I snapped. "They stand right on my rink when they come to the trough."

"Maybe you should have thought of that when you built your rink," she said nonchalantly.

I did not give up. I spent a great deal of my spare time out there on that little patch of ice trying to clear off as much of the pee, the pie and the road apple as I could, but it was impossible to chip it out without ruining the ice surface. I even tried to shovel off a fresh cow pie, but only succeeded in smearing it around. If I was going to learn to skate, it would have to be around the obstacles.

I spent hours out on that little rink, going round and round with my eyes glued to the ice, keeping a wary eye out for the many hazards that dotted its surface. It got so I was even able to keep one leg up in the air, behind me, for an entire lap of the rink without hitting a pie or an apple. I even practised my jumping over a cow pie or a mound of frozen pee. If I had to say so myself, I was getting pretty good.

"C'mon Mom," I urged, for I knew that I could skate as well on that little patch of ice as I could in the big arena in Edson. "You've got to see me. I can really figure skate now."

"Okay," she replied, "as soon as you get your chores done, I'll come out and watch you."

"Good," I warbled. "You're gonna see how good I am now, Mom. You'll see."

I rushed through my chores. I was so excited that Mom was going to come and watch me do my turns on the little patch of ice. When I had completed my chores Mom and my brother and sisters came outside to watch.

I was pretty proud as I laced on my old hand-me-downs and strode towards the rink.

The surface of the ice was still pretty rough, but I had learned how to navigate it. I was able to sail around the ice, on both blades and ankles, as I warmed up. I congratulated myself on how easily I jumped each and every obstacle protruding from the ice.

Then to everyone's surprise, I leaned forward and threw my arms straight out from my body. At this moment I knew I resembled an airplane in full flight. Keeping a close eye on the ice, I kicked my right leg out behind me and glided around the little rink on my left leg.

On one leg I expertly picked my way around each and every cow pie and past the road apples, before cleverly skirting the latest mound of pee. I was the picture of grace and beauty skating on the only ice surface on the stump farm. I gratefully acknowledged my audience, but not until I had stopped skating as the pies and apples really posed too much of a hazard. They all clapped and cheered so I repeated the performance. There was no doubt about it, I was pretty darned good.

When the exhibition was over my sister Gwen stayed outside while the rest returned to the house. "I can jump real good, too," I advised her.

"I betcha can't," she replied.

"Sure I can. I'll show you," I countered. "I just need something to jump over, that's all."

"Why don't you get a block of wood?"

"That's no good. It's too small," I responded. "I need something bigger then that." I looked around for something that was more challenging than a block of wood. Something that was up to my advanced abilities.

"There's nothing else here," Gwen observed as she too scanned the yard for a jumpable object.

"I know," I said excitedly. "I'll jump over you."

"Oh no, you won't," she snapped. "I'm not going to stand out there and let you charge into me."

"No, you don't stand out here. You lay down on the ice and I'll jump over you that way. Just the same way that guy jumped over the barrels in the carnival. C'mon," I urged her, "you lay down right here and I'll jump over you."

Reluctantly she agreed and walked out onto the ice surface and lay down on her back. I circled the rink a couple of times to build up speed, then turned towards the centre of the ice and Gwen laying there flat on her back.

I could just picture myself sailing over her body and landing on one foot on the other side. Would Mom ever be surprised when we told her that I had jumped right over Gwen. At just the right moment I planted one foot and pushed off into a mighty leap.

I lifted my lead skate high to insure that I cleared her. With the other skate, I kicked Gwen right in the side of the head. The blade hit her just below the eye and I sprawled over her and into the snow bank at the side of the rink. I looked back at Gwen who was sitting up holding her head, blood flying everywhere. As I helped Gwen into the house, I thought this was not the surprise I had in mind for Mom.

Maybe I could get back on with the Milky Way crew next year, I thought as I washed the blood from my hands. The Olympics would just have to wait.

THE GREAT SLEIGH RACE

The clomping and prancing of horses' hooves on the packed snow and ice and the sound of sleigh bells on a winter day was a common occurrence on the south road in the 1940s. Horses and sleighs were the preferred mode of transportation and for good reason.

Starting a vehicle in the winter time was a major undertaking. Because the radiator had to be drained each night, water, preferably hot water, had to be replaced every morning. To turn the motor over, someone, usually the strongest or the one who possessed the weakest mind, would have to crank it. This was accomplished by inserting the crank, a length of metal rod bent to the proper shape, into the end of the crankcase at the front of the motor and giving it a good crank. Reluctant motors would sometimes kick back, causing many a sprained wrist or broken finger.

Yes, the horse and sleigh was by far the more desirable mode of transportation, particularly in the winter. There was never any fear of a horse freezing up if left to stand for a spell and they never ran off the road. If the driver encountered a storm or some other unpredictable occurrence, the horse could always be depended upon to find its way home. It was a known fact that the horse would always find his barn where there was shelter and food.

It was a cloudy, snowy winter evening in early December and the gods had willed that two of the south road's senior residents would be leaving Edson at the same time. Each driver had a single horse and each horse was harnessed and pulling a cutter.

Above the tinkling of the sleigh bells and the crunch of hooves on the packed snow and ice came the sound of a heavily accented male voice.

"Hey peeg farmer!" The greeting echoed through the frozen town.

Grandfather looked behind to see who was hollering.

"Well, I'll be…it's Nick the Dog Man, I wonder what the old coot wants," he said, reining in his horse. Grandfather's cutter, loaded with kids and grandkids, slid to a halt as the horse's shod hoofs bit into the roadway.

"Hey, peeg farmer, I'm talking at you," Nick the Dog Man yelled again. "What'sa matter you? You deaf or someting?"

"You bellerin' at me, boy?" Grandfather asked. It was his way of returning the greeting. Even old Nick, who was probably older than Grandfather, was called boy.

"Yes. Yes. You peeg farmer," laughed Nick the Dog Man. "Who you think I'm talking to, you crazy old man? You see anybody else on this road? Hey peeg farmer, can that plug you call a horse run or are you taking it home for peeg feed?"

Oh boy, I thought, as my eyes shifted from Nick the Dog Man to Grandfather. Grandfather was not one to take an insult lightly and Nick the Dog Man had just hurled a fistful. I watched and waited for Grandfather to respond.

"Whose horse are you calling a plug?" roared Grandfather. "That bag of bones that you drive doesn't have enough meat on it to feed one of your mutts. You get that reject from the glue factory outta town before they throw you in jail for treatin' that animal so badly."

"I have never seen such a sorry sight in my life. It hurt my eye to see such a ting," countered Nick the Dog Man, grinning from ear to ear. "A broken-down plug, dragging a sleigh full of kids through the snow with an old man humped over in the seat. You should feed that plug to your peegs. Don't bring it to my place, my dogs, they won't eat such a scrawny 'ting. Har har har," he laughed as he drew his cutter alongside Grandfather's.

"Your dogs are like that nag you call a horse," Grandfather snorted indignantly. "They're all skin and bones, they would eat anything. Never have I seen so many ribs sticking out. Lookit that poor animal, he looks like a picket fence."

Both men were leaving Edson at the end of a short winter's day and heading for home down the south road, and both were engaged in their usual good-natured banter insulting each other and their horses.

Grandfather would often say that he preferred the horse and sleigh in the winter even though he had a truck. "The horse is more dependable in the winter and it don't freeze up," Grandfather would say.

Dad would often counter with, "That usually means that Grandfather was unable to get the truck started today." Nick the Dog Man didn't have a car and always used a horse, winter or summer.

There were times when as chance would have it Nick the Dog Man and Grandfather would be coming home from Edson at the same time with their horse and cutters. When such encounters occurred, one would start a conversation by insulting the other one and his horse. Invariably this verbal sparring would end with one issuing a challenge that would quickly be accepted and the inevitable sleigh race would be on.

"Hey peeg farmer. Maybe I should hitch my stallion to your rig and pull you home," laughed Nick the Dog Man.

"Stallion," Grandfather replied in disgust. "Stallion. That sorry hunk of horse flesh hasn't enough strength to climb a step, let alone a mare. You stay out of my way or I'll run you into the snow."

Fortunate would be the kids who were returning home from school when Grandfather was returning from Edson. For those kids would get a ride, a real treat, a break from the daily two-mile trek home each day. On these days Grandfather's sleigh would often be packed with kids. On days when we encountered only Nick the Dog Man and his sleigh, we were never offered a ride, nor would we have accepted one if it had been offered. No, there was enough fear just knowing that Nick the Dog Man was around and his dogs might be near.

"Hey, leetle boys, leetle girls. You come ride with old Nick, eh. Take peety on your poor old Papa's horse, look at heem, he is so tired. Come. Come leetle ones. Ride with Nick and his magnificent stallion. Come now, I take you all the way home."

I looked quickly at Grandfather then back at Nick the Dog Man. I wasn't sure about the rest of the kids, but I knew I wasn't getting off Grandfather's sleigh and onto Nick the Dog Man's sleigh for anything. A quick glance at the rest of the kids and the fear in their eyes told me they felt the same way.

"Ha," roared Grandfather. "All the way home, eh? That nag of yours will be lucky to get to the railroad crossing. Then these poor kids would have to walk and carry you, too."

"Come children, come ride with Nick, eh," he urged gently.

When those two raced, Nick the Dog Man would sometimes take those unfortunate enough to be told by Grandfather to ride with Nick the Dog Man. Otherwise we didn't go near him, for fear of being eaten by his dogs. Nick had the same reputation as his dogs. It had earned him a great deal of respect, fear and at all times a wide berth.

If you happened to be on Grandfather's sleigh, a race was always filled with fun and excitement. Everyone would be laughing, yelling, singing or whistling. Grandfather was a fun-loving character with a devil-may-care attitude. Grandfather would never pass up an opportunity to try to best his fellow man in a friendly competition.

However, if you were on Nick the Dog Man's sleigh, the race took on an entirely different perspective. To say that you lived in fear of being eaten by either him or his dogs would be an understatement. Those on Nick the Dog Man's sleigh hung on for dear life. Some closed their eyes and prayed. Some cried and prayed. Some sat there like zombies and prayed. The chance meeting would bring out a side of Nick the Dog Man that was otherwise never seen. Suddenly Nick the Dog Man, the old bachelor, the feared recluse, would be transformed into a fun-loving, jovial character. When the opportunity arose, he would never let Grandfather leave town uncontested.

Grandfather designated those who would be riding with Nick the Dog Man. I breathed a sigh of relief as I watched the unfortunates reluctantly climb off of Grandfather's sleigh and onto Nick the Dog Man's.

"Stay clear, you old coyote. I don't want to see you get hurt. Yahoo! Giddyup," Grandfather yelled as soon as everyone was on Nick the Dog Man's sleigh. Grandfather slapped the reins across the horse's backside. "Hang on kids, this is man's stuff now. We'll see who has a real horse," he bellowed at Nick the Dog Man.

When the reins slapped down on its rump, Grandfather's horse immediately reacted to the message. Instantly both horses were at a full gallop as they changed gears and charged forward. The race was on.

Out of Edson they raced, each shouting

encouragement to their charges, each throwing insults at the other. Neck-and-neck the horses would gallop, heading east on 4th Avenue, past the few houses scattered along Highway 16. The horses' manes were flowing and their tails streaming out behind as the snow from their flying hoofs sprayed on the sleighs and their occupants. The bells on the harness would be ringing loudly. The air was filled with the sound of cheering, laughter, bells and the shouting of the two men. Electricity was in the air. It was an exciting time, being a part of the race, yes, this was living.

The horses were fairly evenly matched and the lead changed regularly as they galloped out of town. Nick the Dog Man, his horse and cutter pulled ahead, not much, just a smidgen of a lead it was and he felt it was his duty to heap a few more insults on his adversary.

"What's the matter peeg farmer, you want I should get out and push you? Ha ha ha," he laughed. His passengers, the unfortunate ones, were hanging on for dear life. I looked from face to face. It was predictable, I chuckled. On pallid faces, there were eyes closed tightly, on others there were eyes as wide as saucers. They were all terrified. There was no doubt that they feared for their lives, but the question remained: Was it Nick the Dog Man they feared, was it his dogs or was it the race? Maybe it was all three.

What better way to belittle one's opponent then to pretend to ignore him during the heat of the race. That is exactly what Grandfather did to Nick the Dog Man. He didn't respond to the insults thrown his way, he just smiled at us and winked and never said a word. Then as his horse pulled ahead, he celebrated, but not with insults, with a song. Grandfather's favourite was a song that contained the words, "and under her belly I saw the blue sky". I'm sure they were the only words he knew and he warbled them at the top of his lungs. Oh yes, when he was in the lead Grandfather could sure belt that one out.

East on Highway 16, the spruce and pine trees that lined the highway seemed to fly past as the horses galloped along. Around the bend in the road then south towards the CNR tracks they sped, neither horse slowing. Neither driver gave any quarter. It was a race to the finish.

The railroad crossing was drawing near and I waited. I never really knew what to expect for it was always an exciting time in the race. Highway 16 was cut through the tall pine and spruce trees that grew close to the edge of the highway. Edson was a main switch yard and there was often a train approaching or on the crossing and lengthy delays were not uncommon. The anxiety of whether or not there would be a train coming down the tracks was always present and it added to the excitement. With the noise from Grandfather and Nick the Dog Man urging their horses on, horses' hooves pounding on the frozen road, sleigh bells ringing and kids cheering, trains could not always be heard. More than once there was panic to stop the horse from racing out in front of the train.

"Never say whoa in a horse race," Grandfather yelled as we approached the tracks. On this day we were lucky. There was no train and the sleighs bounced and jumped over the rough tracks. More excitement and joy for the riders.

Immediately across the tracks, the south road made a sharp turn to the right. Neither driver slowed as the approach suddenly appeared before them. At a gallop the horses, sleighs, drivers and kids approached the sharp turnoff.

As the horses turned sharply and headed south, the sleighs would skid towards the snow bank and the ditch on the left side of the road.

Grandfather's horse had the inside track going around the turn. But once more the horses were neck and neck. The sleighs bumped into each other as they skidded crazily from side to side. There were no eyes closed now, in either sleigh. Those of us in Grandfather's sleigh were laughing and shouting encouragement to Grandfather and his horse. Those in Nick the Dog Man's sleigh were scared stiff as their eyes darted in every direction, pleading for help.

Nick the Dog Man's sleigh would probably have gone into the deep snow and the ditch by itself, but a little push from Grandfather's sleigh sent it right off the road. Snow was flying in every direction as Nick the Dog Man's horse broke and started to jump, trying to get back to the road. Now the unfortunates had one more worry. They all leaned way back to avoid the flying hoofs and snow. Fortunately, it was snow that ended up in the face of the occupants of Nick the Dog Man's sleigh.

"I told you to keep out of my way or I'd run you over," yelled Grandfather as he gained the lead and broke into song, "and under her belly I saw the blue sky."

Nick the Dog Man fought to keep his sleigh upright

and out of the ditch. He lost valuable ground and he and his riders could only watch as Grandfather's sleigh blew past and flew down the south road.

The horses with their nostrils flaring continued to follow the drivers' urging. Onward they charged at a dead gallop. Neither driver asked any quarter or gave any. Down the south road into the gully and up the hill on the other side, the horses raced, heading for home.

Grandfather was shouting encouragement to his charge and the fortunate kids were screaming and yelling as they cheered him on.

Nick the Dog Man was cursing Grandfather for running him off the road as he chased after the departing rig. I knew the unfortunates on Nick the Dog Man's sleigh were praying that his dogs would suddenly go deaf and not hear the approaching racket. But we all knew that was not to be, for the noise that accompanied the racers alerted everyone, including Nick the Dog Man's dogs, that there was plenty of activity coming down the road. We could hear them hone their voices long before we arrived.

To the relief of his passengers, Nick the Dog Man stopped the cutter at his driveway to let the kids off. He never went farther than his place and the howling dogs. As Grandfather raced away, Nick the Dog Man's passengers bailed off and hit the road running, running for their lives. Happy to have survived the race. Happy to get away from Nick the Dog Man. Praying that they wouldn't be caught by his dogs.

"I told you to feed that bag of bones to your dogs. He can't run. Look at him, he's dead tired. My horse is still going strong. Would you like to buy a good horse?

I know where you can get one. Giddyup, boy. 'And under her belly I saw the blue sky'," Grandfather would roar triumphantly.

The race was really over at Nick the Dog Man's place. But in reality it would never end. There was never a winner or a loser, but a friendly rivalry between two old men who loved the thrill of the challenge, who loved life. And for the kids who got to ride in the sleighs, there was something to talk about, something to wait for, for we knew that the next time they met in town, there would be another race.

HALF A DOG
IS BETTER THAN NO DOG!

"Bobby!"

I cringed at the sound of Mom's voice calling my name for the umpteenth time. "Bobby, I told you, I want this mess cleaned up and I mean right now, young man. This is the last time I'm going to talk to you about it. You wanted a dog and you got a dog. Now, you get yourself in here and take care of it."

I cursed Bunny, the little black puppy that was running around the house dropping little piles of dog pooh and piddling everywhere it stopped.

I thought back to the assortment of pets that I had while living on the stump farm and how I had longed for this day. The day when I had a dog of my own. After all, I would always argue, every farm boy should have a dog. A dog that would always be there when needed. I would walk out to the barn, into the field or work my trapline and my dog, my trusty companion, would be there, following me. Walking along at my heels. I knew that if I had a dog, we would be true friends, inseparable.

Yes, a dog would certainly be better than the other animals that I had called my pets.

Let me see, I thought as I began the never-ending task of wiping dog pee off the linoleum, there was Rocky. Yes, I remember Rocky real well. The first time I had seen Rocky was when an old 'cluck' had suddenly reappeared after being missing for several days. She came walking back into the yard with a dozen little chicks scurrying around her feet. They were a variety of colours, all peeping and cheeping as they ran after insects that she scratched up from the dirt and grass.

Rocky had been the most colourful of all the chicks. Each of us kids got to pick one chick that we could call our own. I choose the multicoloured chick, he was to be my pet. Grandfather said he was "probably a Rock Island Red" because he was so colourful. I had no idea what a Rock Island Red was, or even if there was such a thing as a Rock Island Red, but Grandfather said it was a Rock Island Red, so Rock Island Red it was and Rocky was his name. Rocky was by far the prettiest chick.

If I would have had another alternative, Rocky certainly wouldn't have been my choice for a pet. Unlike this stupid pup, Rocky was outside in the yard every day and did not take much care or attention, for he was watched over very closely by a jealous guarding old hen. If I was real quick, I could sometimes get him away from the 'cluck' and play with him for awhile. For the next few weeks, I watched as Rocky grew from a tiny chick into a very strapping young rooster. Rocky was no longer a cute little pet, he was the cock of the walk as he strutted around the farmyard, but he was still my pet.

I will never forget the day that Mom announced to the rest of the family. "Tonight we can thank Bobby for this fine supper," she stated as she placed a roaster of fried chicken on the table.

Nobody could cook chicken like Mom could. Today, the house was full of tantalizing aromas as she browned the pieces of chicken — pieces that earlier in the day had been a complete Rocky — in a frying pan. Once Rocky was browned to her satisfaction, she coated each piece with a mixture of spices and flour and placed him in the roaster. Rocky was smothered with onions, and the roaster popped into the oven. There he roasted until he was tender and delicious. A tasty morsel to the end.

Yes, the family could thank me for dinner. I had raised Rocky from a small chick to a large healthy young rooster. Because Dad was away working at the time, I, being 'the man of the house', had caught Rocky the rooster and had stretched his neck across the chopping block. Then with one swish of the axe, his head remained on the block, while the rest of Rocky flopped and flapped around the yard. It was his final run. 'The man of the house' then got to dip the carcass into a pot of boiling water and pluck the feathers from the bird. Mom performed the rest of the tasks required before supper was served.

Yes, Rocky had been my pet for a few short weeks that summer, but like the rest of the chicks, Rocky had ended up on the supper table. I could almost feel the smug smiles of my brother and sisters as they chewed into Rocky. Each of us had picked a chick from the 'clucks' brood when she had first walked back into the yard. Whenever we had chicken for supper, I, being 'the man of the house', the Chief Chicken Chopper, got to make the decision on which bird would fill the roaster and grace our table. Much to the chagrin of my siblings, the other chicks, their pets, had already fallen under the axe. Rocky had been the last to go. Such was the life of a pet chicken on the stump farm.

As I moved to the next puddle of pee, I thought of Runt, another pet that had stayed with us for a short time, albeit somewhat longer then Rocky. Runt had been born into a large litter of pigs on Grandfather's pig farm. Runt had been just a little guy at birth, and was not deemed worthy.

"Can't waste any of the sow's milk on that runt," Grandfather had said. "He'll never make it to market. The way I look at it, I can either knock it on the head right now or one of the kids can have it and see if they can raise it."

Runt was a little pink piglet and truly a runt. He was about half the size of the other piglets in the litter. With an awful lot of care, and I might add a tremendous amount of time and patience on Mom's part, Runt did make it. Runt had the run of the yard once he got big enough to romp around. Oh yes, Runt was a fine pet, a real success story and without the competition from the rest of the brood, Runt not only survived, but he grew faster and bigger than the other piglets in the litter. I would remind Grandfather regularly that Runt was bigger then the piglets he had kept.

"That's good, boy," Grandfather would reply. "You make sure you take good care of the pig now."

Runt quickly became a good-sized pet and was soon relegated to a pen down by the barn. There Runt stayed until one fateful day when Grandfather showed up. It was time for Runt to pay for the good life he had been living.

"C'mon boy," Grandfather called to me. "Let's get this pig loaded onto the truck. C'mon, now, I haven't got all day." Grandfather backed the truck down to the pen and Runt was herded up the chute. Runt didn't object to being loaded like the pigs on Grandfather's place did. He was used to a lot of human contact. Being led around by kids (me) was all part of being a pet. Runt quickly ran up the chute and stood there waiting for a ride.

Today, I was not 'the man of the house'. Dad was home, but I was part of the team and I got to accompany Grandfather, Dad and Runt. We left the stump farm and drove north on the south road, north to Grandfather's place. It was butchering day and it was Runt's last ride.

Several pigs took their last ride that day, but because Runt was included and Runt had been my pet, I got the privilege of helping. Once Runt had been dispatched, I helped to hoist him into the air and dunk him into the barrel of boiling water. The boiling water helped to loosen the bristle. Then Runt was stretched out on a table and it was my job to scrape every inch of Runt's carcass to remove the bristle so that Dad and Grandfather could get him ready for winter.

Once again, I had helped supply food for our table.

Runt, my pet, was a big part of our winter's larder. Runt was destined to be the ham and bacon.

Bunny joined me and tugged at my pant leg as I crawled over to the next puddle. The happy little black puppy reminded me of another pet. Mrs. Sliva, who lived on the dairy farm south of our place, had given Larry and I each a baby rabbit, two little tiny bunnies, to have as pets. My rabbit was a wee little black-and-white guy and he was so small, he would fit right into the palm of my hand. I remembered the day that I had laid a piece of lettuce in my palm and was letting the little guy eat it. With those big teeth of his, he took a good hunk of skin right out of my hand, but that was all right, he was my pet.

The little rabbit was the only pet that was allowed to sleep in the house. I recalled having asked Mom, "Can I take him to bed with me?"

"I don't think that would be such a good idea," Mom replied. "He's pretty little to be in bed with a big boy like you. Just think what would happen to him if you or Larry rolled over on him."

"He'll be okay, Mom," I assured her.

"I don't think so," she said. "We'll put him in a box at the foot of the bed. He'll do just fine there."

"But Mom," I protested.

"The rabbit stays in the box, at the foot of the bed, or he stays outside," Mom said sternly.

"Well, he can't stay outside," I grumbled. "The coyotes will eat him."

"Then he stays in the box at the foot of the bed."

I got up several times to check on the little guy. He was huddled in one corner of the cardboard box beside

Larry's rabbit. My rabbit looked like he was more scared and cold then Larry's. I waited until Mom had gone to bed and I was sure that everyone was asleep. Then as quiet as a mouse, I slipped out of bed, crept over to the box and gently scooped the little rabbit out. Holding him close to my chest I returned to bed, to my nice warm bed. The little rabbit worked his way under the covers and snuggled up close to me. I slept soundly, knowing that my little rabbit was a warm little rabbit. He was with someone who loved him and would protect him.

I bounced out of bed when Mom called in the morning. It was time to do chores. I had slept so soundly, I had even forgotten about the little rabbit.

"Where's your rabbit?" Mom asked when I walked into the kitchen.

"I...uh...he's..." I stuttered.

"He's not in the box," Mom assured me.

"He's...uh...he's..."

"He's in the bed, isn't he?" Mom said, glaring at me.

"Uh huh," I mumbled.

"That's fine," Mom replied. "You had your chance. Tonight the rabbit sleeps outside with the rest of the animals."

"What happened to Rob's bunny?" asked Larry as he walked into the room.

"Your brother didn't listen too well last night," Mom replied. "The rabbit's in the bed and I want it out of there right now."

"He's squashed flat," Larry replied.

"You killed my rabbit," I shouted at him when I heard this startling news.

41

"I did not," he protested. "He's on your side of the bed and he's flatter than a pancake."

"I told you not to take that rabbit to bed," Mom admonished me. "You probably rolled over on him during the night, and that poor little rabbit was too small to get out of your way."

"What am I going to do now?" I asked with tears in my eyes.

"Well, he's too small to eat, so you might as well throw him out on the garbage pile," Mom replied. "Maybe the next time you'll listen and do what you're told."

As I moved over to clean up a pile of dog crap, the little puppy was busy sniffing around my hands. "I should rub your nose in this," I growled at her.

"Don't you touch her," Judy sniped at me. "I own half that dog, too."

"Well, she'll never learn to go outside if you don't train her properly," I snapped back.

"You can do what you want with your half of the dog, but you better leave my half of the dog alone," she warned me.

"How come I have to share a dog anyway?" I asked Mom. "Why can't I have my own dog?"

"Because we're only going to have one dog around this house," Mom replied. "Don't forget, Grandfather gave the puppy to your sister. You should be thankful that she agreed to share her puppy with you. She didn't have to do that, you know."

"I know," I grumbled, thinking back to the day Grandfather brought the little puppy to the house. I thought for sure, being the oldest, I would get the puppy, but no. Grandfather gave her to my sister Judy and she was the youngest. She didn't even know how to treat a dog; she gave it a stupid name like Bunny.

But Judy was not selfish or greedy and she readily agreed to share her puppy with me. Well, maybe Bunny wasn't such a stupid name after all. The little black puppy wasn't much bigger than a little bunny. No, Bunny was an okay name, I thought at the time.

Judy and I would sit for hours playing with our puppy. However, petting the puppy did cause the odd ruckus.

"You're only supposed to pet your half of the puppy," Judy would scold me, whenever I touched the dog's head. You see, Judy had given me the back half of the puppy. She had retained ownership of the front half. The half that ate and yipped, the half that would lick your hand. I was given the back half, the half that pooped and peed all over the floor.

I looked at the little black puppy bouncing around. There was no comfort in growing up and learning the facts of life, I thought as I wiped up the last puddle. The life expectancy of a pet, on the Stump Farm, was very short. Very short indeed, I thought as the little black puppy squatted and another puddle formed. The back half of this puppy probably wouldn't be around long, either.

FIRE IN THE HOLE, ROB

Life on the stump farm could never be described as easy, but for all the hardships there were many happy days. Other than the big town of Edson, we didn't know there was any other life, pleasures or luxuries than that to which we had been born into. After all, we had a roof over our heads, there was always something to eat and there was plenty of wood for the cook-stove. Even marginal land provided enough to keep a family alive and well, as long as Dad worked all winter in the bush camps, that is.

One day there was change in the air. There was excitement, the likes of which had not been seen on the stump farm since the day we moved into the brand new log house. The excitement started to build shortly after Dad had snagged a full-time job. From now on he would be working in Edson, in the round house. No longer would he be working away from home, spending months at a time in the logging camps north of Edson. Yes sirree, lady luck had smiled on the Adams family and Dad had landed a biggie. He was going to work as a machinist for the Canadian National Railways. Full-time employment meant a monthly paycheque, something that those of us living on the stump farm had very little knowledge of, because we had always lived from day to day.

However, Mom had a pretty good idea of what a monthly cheque was and what it meant. She wasted no time whatsoever in making her feelings known. A regular monthly paycheque was a ticket to bigger and better things. Yes, change was in the air, we could all feel it. We could all draw from Mom's change in attitude; we could feel the electricity as the excitement mounted.

"I think I've had about enough of barely existing out here on this worthless piece of land," Mom declared one night at the supper table. "Heaven only knows, I've swatted enough mosquitoes and plowed through enough mud to last me a lifetime. I think it's time we looked for something different, some easier times. Maybe we could have a little better life, like…well, like moving into Edson would be a good start."

"Edson?" came the uniform response as we all sat up and took notice. "Why would we want to move into Edson?" I asked. This was a real bombshell. Since we had moved from Wildwood, we had never lived in a town nor, to my knowledge, had it ever been considered. To me, a town was a place where city folks lived and where country folks visited on Saturdays, but that was only to go to a picture show or get groceries and then get out, out to the peace and quiet of the country. Town was no place to dally. Towns ranked right up there with the outhouse when it came to dallying. Go in, do your business and get out. Towns were not a place where good respectable country folk chose to spend their time.

However, Mom had surely rippled the waters with her supper-time statement. It looked suspiciously like the perception of towns in the Adams household was about to change. Towns, particularly Edson, were suddenly being looked at in an entirely different light as they loomed large in our future.

It was a major event the day the family traveled to Edson, "just for a look-see," Mom had informed us. "It's always a good idea to take a look at what's available before making a major decision like moving," Mom said. "After all, one just doesn't pull up stakes and move without giving it some serious thought."

Our first stop was on the west side of town. There Mom just happened to spot a vacant lot, a very tiny vacant lot that appeared to have all the attributes necessary for a new house. Actually the lot was covered with long grass. There was even one little tree, a poplar, to remind us of the farm.

"What do you think?" Mom asked as we stood on the postage-stamp-sized lot on 7th Avenue. "I think it's perfect. It has everything we want. It's just perfect, isn't it?"

"Well Florence, if you like it, then I guess it looks alright to me, too," Dad replied, not wanting to rain on Mom's parade.

"How can it be perfect?" I asked. "There's nothing here. There's no trees, there's just a bunch of houses."

"What do you mean, you don't like it?" Mom asked, looking both surprised and hurt. "There's a nice tree, and over here," she said, pointing to the west, "look at all the spruce trees. There's lot's of trees."

"Well, I don't care, I don't like it," I replied. "There'll be nothing to do here. I won't be able to go hunting or trapping. There'll be nothing to do."

"Sure you will," Mom replied. "Look, there's no houses to the west. We're right on the edge of the bush here. Why, I'll bet those trees are full of squirrels and chickens."

"I doubt it," I replied. "Just look at it, it's all muskeg and swamp spruce. I'll bet there'll be just as many mosquitoes here as there is at the farm. Anyway, this lot is way too small."

"Well, town lots aren't very big," Mom replied. "And there's mosquitoes everywhere, you're never going to get away from mosquitoes. But we won't have to fight that mud every time it rains."

"I don't like it," I informed everybody.

"I think it's just perfect. You'll be closer to school, you can come home every day for lunch. You'll be able to do many things that you haven't been able to do on the farm. I know you're just going to love it here," Mom stated.

"But Mom, I won't be able to trap squirrels or cut any telephone poles," I replied. "How am I going to make any money?"

"You can get a paper route or set pins at the bowling alley," Mom replied. "How long do you think it will take you to put a house up?" Mom asked Dad.

"Well, it shouldn't take too long, if everyone helps," he replied.

"That settles it then," Mom stated and a big satisfied grin crossed her face. "I guess we all better get busy then, because I'm not spending another winter on the farm. I want to be in my new house before the snow flies."

"You mean we're moving?" I asked. "Just like that? Don't we haveta buy the lot first?"

"Just like that," Mom replied. "I knew everyone was just going to love this lot so I already bought it. Now the sooner we get started, the sooner we get the house built and the sooner we can move into it."

"But I thought we were just coming to look at this lot," I protested.

"Well, you've looked at it, now it's time to get busy and build on it. There's more to this world than that useless piece of farm land. You'll soon learn that in town there are more opportunities, more things to see and do. Your future is in town, there's no future on that farm," Mom replied.

Suddenly, I realized that old stump farm had become a major part of my life. I got a real sick feeling in the pit of my stomach as I thought about all the things in my world that were coming to an end. The more I thought about it, the more I realized I didn't really mind milking the cows, not even the kicker. Feeding the chickens, cutting and splitting firewood or drawing water were only minor irritations. I wouldn't even complain if I had to be 'the man of the house' again. I was even going to miss Nick the Dog Man's dogs. In fact, the more I thought about them, the more

I realized those dogs weren't really that bad, they just barked a lot. I had even got used to the mud. I had learned to walk on the side of the ditch and hadn't lost any rubber boots in a long time. No, moving into Edson was not high on my list of priorities. Already I was longing for the familiarity of the stump farm and dreading the thought of the unknown.

That summer, Dad worked two jobs, midnight shifts at the round house and days at the new home in Edson. Long before the snow flew, he had enough of the house finished so that we could move into two rooms. Come rain or shine that summer, Dad sawed boards with a hand saw and we nailed them. We soon found out what everyone in Edson already knew. Edson had just as many mosquitoes as there were on the farm, and when it rained, Edson had just as much mud as the south road. Man, I spent so much of the summer soaked to the skin, it seemed like it rained every day.

We had been in the house in Edson for a few days and the rains came again. It had rained for a couple of days and finally the sun had popped through the heavy black clouds. A warm sunny day followed. The air was heavy with humidity and the fresh clean smell that always follows rain. Though it was not as fresh as the farm smelled after a good rain, it was enough to make one forget the trials of urban living.

Some things never change, I thought, as I watched my brother plow through the mud as he came down the back alley. A cloud of mosquitoes swarmed around his head and his rubber boots were caked with thick heavy layers of clay. In fact, his feet looked about the size of water pails as he struggled into the yard.

"Hey kid, ain't life great in the big town? It's a good thing we moved from the farm to get away from the mosquitoes and the mud," I greeted him and laughed. "Why don't you drag your feet through the grass and scrape the mud off your boots?"

"No way Rob, I'm through scraping mud," he informed me. "I've got something here that'll take care of the mud," he replied as we walked around to the front of the house. The mud clung to his boots like it belonged there. During the trek from the alley to the front of the house he never lost even one little chunk of clay.

At the front of the house he stopped by the doorway. Then with a mighty grunt, he hoisted one heavy boot up onto the steps. "Can you get me a match, Rob?" he asked.

"What for?"

"I'm going to get rid of this mud," he replied with a sly grin.

"Sure you are. What're you gonna do, burn it off?" I laughed.

"Nope. I'm going to blow it off," he announced as he pulled a huge red firecracker out of his pocket and held it up for me to see. "I figure this beauty oughta get rid of the mud real quick."

"Wow, you sure you ain't got a stick of dynamite?" I replied. "Where did you get that thing? Here, give it to me, let me look at it."

"No way, and it's not dynamite," he replied. "It's a giant firecracker, and it's mine."

"It sure looks like dynamite to me," I whistled as I looked at that beauty.

"Well, it's not. It's a firecracker, it's mine and I'm gonna blow this mud to kingdom come."

"Come on," I begged. "Just let me have one look at it. I won't steal it from you."

"No way," he replied. "This is my firecracker. If you want one, you can go and buy one for yourself, just like I did."

"Holy cow," I mumbled. "I never saw a firecracker that big in my whole life. Where'd you get it?"

"Downtown," he chuckled. "You know Rob, living in town ain't that bad after all. Mom was right, there is a whole new world out there. I never thought you could just pop down to the store and pick up a firecracker when you got mud on your rubbers. You certainly couldn't do that when you lived on the farm, now could you?"

I had to agree with him there. However, I never had enough money to just pop downtown and buy anything. But that firecracker, it was something else. It looked to be about four inches long and a good half-inch thick. It was a monster.

"That thing looks just like a stick of dynamite," I said.

"Yeah, doesn't it though," he smiled at me. "Will you go get me a match?" he asked again.

"You bet," I replied. I was kicking myself for not having the foresight to have thought of a firecracker to blow the mud off my boots. What a great idea, I thought as I raced into the kitchen and grabbed a box of matches.

Back on the step, I watched, enviously, as Larry carefully pushed the giant firecracker between his boot

51

and the mud. He was in no hurry, he had time on his side and he had the giant firecracker. I was tempted to jump in and help, but I contained myself. I sat there, patiently, waiting and watching while he made sure that the firecracker was placed in just the right spot, where it appeared that the largest amount of mud had accumulated. Inserting the giant firecracker caused the mud to push away from the boot. But it appeared that Larry didn't want to leave anything to chance so he carefully pushed the mud back, packing it tightly, setting the firecracker solidly in place. When he was satisfied that the charge was set to just the right depth and packed as tight to the boot as possible, he nodded to me.

"Okay, Rob, you can touch her off," he said proudly and straightened up to await the de-mudding of his rubber boot.

It was quite a ceremony. I removed one wooden match from the box and held it up for his approval.

"Whattaya think?" I asked, holding the match close to his face.

"Looks like a match to me," he replied very knowledgeably. "I think that little baby just oughta do the trick, whattaya think?"

"I think so too," I agreed. Then I struck the match and held it up to eye level. We both watched as the match flared up. We cast each other a knowing glance and then I leaned over and touched the flame to the fuse.

"Fire in the hole, Rob," Larry sang out as a huge smile lit his face. "Stand back now, I tell you, there's fire in the hole."

Sssttttsssttssttt sputtered the fuse. I watched the little sparks as they flew from the fuse. It was easy to watch the progress of the fire as it spit and sizzled along the fuse towards the business end of the giant firecracker. Ssssstttt…the sputtering stopped when the fire disappeared into the red casing. The silence was unbearable; it seemed to take forever. Then suddenly there was this thunderous explosion.

BOOOOMMMMM! The noise shattered the tranquillity of the quiet neighborhood. I'm sure that it resounded throughout the town.

Even though I knew the bang was coming and I was waiting for it, I was obviously not totally prepared. I recoiled at the sound, falling backward. I slammed into the doorjamb and shut my eyes about the same time as a huge gob of clay splattered on the door beside my ear. I could feel hot spray stinging my face and hands. Various sizes of clumps of mud plastered my pants to my legs. Then, as suddenly as it had erupted, all was quiet. There was not a sound to be heard.

I opened my eyes and looked down at my pants. Oh no, I thought, my pants were covered with mud. I looked over at Larry's foot. It was still on the step exactly where it had been when the firecracker exploded. However, it was no longer covered with clay. Except for a few faint whitish grey streaks, sort of like a sun burst, Larry's rubber boot looked to be about as clean as the day it was bought.

"Holy Mackerel!" I exclaimed as I looked at the mudless boot. "Did that thing ever do a good job. I'm going to get me a whole supply of firecrackers, as soon as I can get my hands on some cash. Look at your shoe, there's no mud on it," I said, looking up at Larry.

Larry wore sort of a sickly smile. He was trying awfully hard to show a brave face, sorta 'how'd you like that?' kinda look, but he wasn't saying anything. As he stood there silently, I could see big ole tears welling up in the corners of his eyes. These were not tears of joy.

Finally he spoke. "My foot don't feel so good, Rob," he said, his voice cracking. Then he sat down on the step and took off his rubber boots. When his foot came out of the blasted rubber boot, it was accompanied by a cloud of steam. Larry got up and slowly limped into the house.

Yes, Mom was right, as Larry had just found out, there was another world beyond the stump farm. I took a seat on the mud-splattered step and settled in to contemplate life on the little lot, town living and Larry's rubber boots. I picked up the one that was now free of mud and looked at it carefully. Steam was still pouring out the top. In all the years on the stump farm, I doubt that Larry had ever suffered as much pain as he was at that minute. Ah, yes, the Adams family had arrived in town, with a thunderous bang.

HAVEN'T YOU EVER SEEN A BOMB?

"What the hell is that?" asked Mom. She had just walked into my bedroom and was staring at my new doorstop.

"It's a bomb," I replied matter-of-factly.

"It's a what?" she asked again, not believing her ears.

"A bomb," I replied. "Haven't you ever seen a bomb?"

"Are you crazy?" she asked.

I laughed, thinking back to how the bomb came to be in our house.

Spread out on my bed were hundreds of shells. I was proudly displaying my collection to some friends, giving them a blow-by-blow description of how I got each one.

"This," I said, picking up a .50 caliber machine gun shell, "was picked up by a soldier in Germany. He brought it back as a souvenir, but he gave it to me cause I've got such a big collection."

"I got a better one than that," said one of my friends, who was obviously not impressed with my machine gun bullet.

"So have I," I replied. I had been saving my best until they were suitably impressed and then I was going to bring it out and lay it on the bed. That would really knock their eyes out. Now was the time to dazzle them.

I pulled out the drawer under the head of my bed as they all watched and waited. Boy, were they in for a big surprise. I reached into the drawer and carefully extracted a 20-millimeter cannon shell.

"This one's from the nose gun of a B-29 bomber," I boasted. "The gunner himself gave it to me." There, I thought to myself as I looked at my challenger. Beat that, smarty!

"That's nothing," he said. "I've got a bomb. In fact I've got two bombs."

"Oh, sure you do," I laughed. "And my aunt's cat has a black ass, too." Everybody laughed at my joke.

"I do too," he said, not laughing.

"Okay, let's go and see them then," I challenged. None of us believed him, but if he did have a bomb, I wanted it.

"I can't show them to anybody," he responded, sort of withdrawing.

"Yeah, well, my aunt don't have a cat, either," I laughed. Then everyone else laughed.

"My dad won't let me show them to anybody. He says they're too dangerous."

"Here," I said, pushing the 20 mm shell across the blanket towards him. "I'll let you touch this one. Then you'll know what real men used in the war."

"Honest, guys. There's two real bombs in our shed," he pleaded to be believed. "But my dad won't let us go near them."

"Well," I kept on pushing, "if you got two bombs in your shed like you say, then you've seen them, right?" I was going to get a look in that shed, just in case there were bombs.

"I've seen them lots of times," he boasted.

"If you've seen them, why can't we see them? Let's all go and have a look at them right now."

"No way."

"Oh yeah, you haven't got any bombs anyway and if you did, then you're too chicken to look at them," one of the others sang out.

"Yeah, all we want is one little look. Then we'll leave."

Finally, he relented and we walked over to his shed to have a look at some real bombs. First he had to check in his house to make sure that his dad wasn't home. The coast was clear and we ran to the shed. It was locked and he had to return to the house to get the key. This was great! We were all real anxious as he pushed the door open and we stared into the darkness.

"It sure is dark in here," someone said as we walked through the door and waited for our eyes to adjust.

This was exciting; my heart was pounding as I followed him over to one corner of the shed. My heart stopped. There before me were the bombs. They were in the corner, standing on their tail fins with their explosive noses pointed towards the sky. They were about eighteen inches long and about four inches in diameter.

My eyes massaged them as they followed the lines from the nose down the body, narrowing to the slender base and finally to the fins that were lodged inside a metal circle. I just stood there looking at them, admiring their beauty.

"I have to pick one up," I said, my hands aching to feel their shiny white surface. I stepped forward.

"Oh no you ain't," he yelled out. "My dad said no one can pick them up."

Oh man, I moaned to myself, they're so close. I'd give anything to be able to put my hands on them for just one little second.

"Well, then I'm gonna touch one."

"You can't touch one, either. My dad said no one can touch them."

"It can't hurt anything and besides he won't know if you don't tell him," I whispered and reached forward. The tips of my fingers barely brushing the white enamel sent a shiver through my body. My fingers stopped. I was touching it! I couldn't believe it, my fingers were actually touching a bomb. The tips of my fingers ever-so-gently caressed the surface. I was startled! It felt real cold and I held my breath, waiting for it to explode. But nothing happened.

"I'm gonna pick it up," I informed my horrified host.

"I'm gonna tell my Dad."

"What're you gonna tell him, that you let us into the

shed when you weren't supposed to?" I answered, never taking my eyes off the bombs.

As I reached down, there was a mad rush for the door and my friends fled the shed. I put one hand on the nose of the bomb and the other on the tapered neck. I felt the rush of adrenaline and my heart was pounding as my fingers closed around the bomb. Man, is this thing ever cold, I thought.

Very gently I lifted it off its resting place on the floor of the shed. It was heavy, a lot heavier than it looked. I was alone in the shed with the most beautiful thing I had ever seen. I felt certain it would soon be the latest addition to my shell collection. Slowly, carefully, I raised it to eye level to admire it.

I turned it over in my hands, admiring the sleek lines. My hand slowly moved along the round firm barrel of the explosive chamber, then gently down the tapered shank and finally to the fins. I admired the unmarred glossy white enamel finish. It was indeed a rare beauty. A once-in-a-lifetime find.

No one had offered me one of these babies, I thought to myself, but this was one prize that I had to have.

I turned it over and I noticed what looked to me like a cotter's pin sticking out of the bomb, right up at the front, near the nose.

"Hey guys," I called to my cowardly friends, "this thing's got a pin in it just like a hand grenade. Come on in and see it." It seemed that they had little desire to come back into the shed with someone holding a bomb.

Since nobody would come in the shed, I decided to take it outside where they could all see it. I held it very carefully. I turned it over and looked at it one more time, being extra careful not to touch the pin. Then carefully, on tiptoes so as not to jar my precious cargo, I started for the door.

My friend was beyond worrying about his dad finding out he had showed us the bombs. When he saw me walking out the door carrying the bomb, his eyes just about bugged right out of his head. He bolted for the safety of the house. No one came near me and they backed away if I approached them.

The bomb was even more beautiful than it had been in the shed. Its solid white enamel glistened even brighter in the sunlight. I was on top of the world. I couldn't believe that I was standing there holding a real live bomb. My heart was pounding as I savoured the moment and ran my hand along the length of the polished surface, slowly turning it.

Suddenly I noticed it, there at the base of the pin. Rust. The pin had rusted at the base. The perfect surface had been marred ever so slightly. It was not much; in the shed it was not noticeable, but out in the sunshine it really stood out against the glossy white surface.

The pin, I thought, had to be the firing mechanism. I wondered what would happen if the pin was removed. I was not too certain that I wanted to find out, but curiosity got the better of me. Slowly, I reached for the pin.

My friends had moved in a little closer, but as soon as I touched that pin they scattered again.

With the tips of my fingers I caressed the pin and tried to wiggle or jiggle it, just a little. I really didn't want the pin to jump out. It didn't move. I gripped it a little firmer and applied a little pressure, trying to turn it to see if it was loose. It held fast; there was no wiggling, jiggling or turning. It was in there solid. Rusted in.

What the heck, I thought, and looked around at my friends who were peeking out from behind buildings.

"Watch this," I yelled and gave the pin my best shot. It was in there pretty solid. It didn't move. Heads disappeared like greased lightning.

I was a little bolder now that I figured I knew how the bomb worked. Holding it by the fin, the explosive end hanging down, I went to work on my friend. I just had to have one of these beauties for my collection. I wouldn't be able to sleep until I had one of those babies tucked into the drawer under my bed. I tried everything I knew to persuade him to give me one. I whined. I sniveled. I begged. I cajoled. But no dice, he held firm and would not part with one. I stayed and pleaded, refusing to leave. Finally, he agreed to let me come back to see them, but only if I promised not to tell his father. I promised. I wanted one of those bombs so bad I ached all over.

The fact that the bombs kept calling me back time after time was evident in that the owner was fast becoming one of my best friends and I was at his place every single day. I would look at the bombs, hold the bombs, caress the bombs. I had to have one of those bombs.

Familiarity did breed contempt. I had handled those bombs so often, as did my friend, that we both began to take them for granted. There was no longer any fear that they would explode. We soon became old pros at handling bombs.

There was no longer any thrill to be gained by walking into the shed, grabbing a bomb and walking out into the daylight to admire it. We needed more excitement in our lives. We could pretend we were bombers flying over Germany. We would bomb the Krauts.

It was easy to fly over Germany carrying the bombs under our arms, but dropping them could be a problem. If they didn't explode they might land on a foot and they were pretty heavy.

"I know," I said, full of excitement at the thought. "Your garden can be Germany, full of Germans. We'll run at the garden holding the bombs above our heads and at the edge of the garden, we'll stop and throw the bombs as far as we can into it. Then we'll turn around and run back behind the shed in case they explode."

"Sounds good to me," he said.

It was time to bomb the Krauts. I hoisted my bomb and once more admired its glossy white finish, the sleekness of its body and the trimness of the fins. Once again it felt strangely cold. I kissed it for good luck, then raised it to the bombing position. I was ready for the mission.

Our bombers took off at the side of the shed and running at top speed with a bomb locked in the bomb bay, over our heads, we charged towards the garden and the enemy lines. Reaching the edge of the garden, we stopped and threw the bombs as far as we could. Then we turned and fled towards the shed and the safety of the base.

The thump of the bombs landing in the garden could be heard long before we got to the shed, but we ran on anyway just in case there were delayed explosions. Sitting behind the shed, we waited for the big bang that never came.

We retrieved the bombs and continued to bomb the Krauts until we were exhausted. Our bombing raids continued for many days, until their garden was pockmarked from the many bombs that had fallen.

One day we were in the middle of a number of bombing raids when there was a different sound. It was not of metal hitting soft dirt. It sounded suspiciously like metal hitting metal. That caused the old adrenaline to pump and we both sped up and zipped around the corner of the shed and waited. Still nothing happened, but it was some time before we got up enough nerve to peer around the side of the shed.

The two bombs were laying there in the garden just as they had been after each raid. We went to examine them. Something had caused the different noise. We approached with extreme caution. One of them had hit a large rock that was buried just below the surface. There was no damage to the rock, but a small chunk of enamel was missing from the bomb.

From this we gained more courage. We picked our next targets. We imagined that the sidewalks were concrete pillboxes where the krauts were hiding. We would bomb the cement sidewalk. We carefully picked out a section of the sidewalk that would be our target. We lined up like two bombers and then ran at the sidewalk. We hurled our bombs at the target then quickly peeled off for the safety of the house, the shed being too far to reach now that we had new targets. Clunk. Clunk. Both bombs bounced off the cement.

We slowly returned to assess the damage. Upon close examination, we noticed that there was only a small amount of enamel scraped off each bomb from the impact. The sidewalk showed no noticeable ill effects.

After the sidewalks, our bombers ran amok. We bombed everything in sight.

The bombs soon lost their appeal and became boring for everyone but me. I still yearned for one. I was not going to quit until I got one—only one—that's all I wanted. I increased the pressure on my friend. Relent and I'll leave was my not-too-subtle message.

Finally, my efforts were rewarded. "I don't feel like bombing any more Krauts," he advised me when I arrived at his place. "My dad says that if you want those bombs, you can have them."

"Both of them?" I asked, unable to believe my ears.

"Both of them," he replied. "Dad said he was glad to be rid of them. They're yours. All you gotta do is take 'em home with you."

I walked into the shed unable to believe my good fortune. My persistence had paid off. I was rewarded with both, not just one. I was ecstatic. I looked at their battered hulls, the enamel chipped and scraped from the many bombing runs. They looked beaten and bruised. I thought back to the first time I had seen them standing in that shed so glossy white and pure. But then they belonged to someone else. Now they were mine and I loved every bit of them, missing enamel and all. They now belonged to me.

I tucked one bomb under each arm and strutted out of the shed and down the street. I was heading for home. It was a glorious day. I pranced into the house and marched straight into my bedroom where I laid them on the bed. I examined them ever so carefully and finally chose one for my collection. It would rest under my bed. The other I stood against the door. It made a perfect doorstop.

Then I dug out the rest of my shells. I wanted to admire the entire collection. I was alone in the room with my coveted prize. I was elated. Now there was no doubt I had the best shell collection around.

I was in the process of sorting out my collection when Mom walked in and noticed the bomb doorstop.

"What the hell is that?" asked Mom. She had just walked into my bedroom and was staring at my new doorstop.

"It's a bomb," I replied matter-of-factly.

"It's a what?" she asked again, not believing her ears.

"A bomb," I replied. "Haven't you ever seen a bomb?"

"Are you crazy? And that?" asked Mom as she walked further into my room and saw the other bomb laying on my bed.

"They're bombs," I proudly proclaimed as I lifted the bomb and held it up for Mom to get a closer look.

"Have you lost your mind?" she yelled as she grabbed me and bolted from the room.

"They're bombs, Mom," I said proudly, clutching my baby, "and they're mine."

ALIENS

I was no stranger to the streets of Edson. It had been nearly a year since the Adams family had pulled up stakes, leaving the stump farm, the muskeg, the swamp spruce, tamarack and willows, the mosquitoes, horse flies, deer flies, wasps and no-see-ums behind. Now, we lived in Edson, on the west side of town, at the end of 7th Avenue, right next to another muskeg, with more swamp spruce, tamarack and willows, more mosquitoes, horse flies, deer flies, wasps and no-see-ums.

I swatted at a mosquito that had hounded me incessantly as I limped off the sidewalk, away from the street lights. I entered the darkness and took a short cut through a vacant lot behind the medical clinic.

Unlike the stump farm, there was no need to carry a lantern or flashlight on the streets of Edson as they were well lit. There was a light standard on every corner and often another in the middle of the block. When lights were on in a home, open windows and doors also provided varying degrees of illumination. But the alleys were different. In the hours of darkness the alleys were a mixture of shadows, one seemingly darker than the other.

But to me, it mattered not whether I walked the streets and alleys in the middle of the day or the dark of night. For I had become very familiar with them all, thanks to my entrepreneurial skills. I knew every house, shed, garage and garbage can. The town of Edson had been a good place to live and it was very profitable. Who would have dreamed that in less than a year a country boy could have fared so well in the big town?

I was one of the fortunate few who had snagged a job setting pins at the bowling alley. "You get a nickel a line," advised the man when he hired me. "Miss one night and I give the job to one of the other boys. There's lots of boys hanging around here looking for a job, you know."

"You can count on me, sir," I replied. Wow, I thought to myself, a whole nickel a line. I looked around the room. I was going to smile at the other boys who were standing around trying to get this plum of a job. One other kid, Billy, was walking towards the end of the building. I knew he was one of the pin-setters. There was no one else standing around, or sitting for that matter. I guessed that the others, the ones dying for this great job, would be in later. Boy, would they be surprised when they found out that I, the early bird, had scooped the job, I chuckled.

"Well, you ready to go to work, boy?" the man asked gruffly.

"Yessir, I am."

"Well, go on then, get on down there," he instructed and pointed to the far end of the alley where Billy had disappeared behind the wall.

"Sir," I stuttered as he turned to walk away. "What's a line?"

"You mean you don't know what a line is?" he replied and looked a little shocked. "You ever bowled?"

"No, sir," I muttered.

"Well, boy," he replied and shook his head. "You see, each time a person bowls a game, it's recorded across the score sheet and we call that a line. Now you get on down there. Billy will show you what to do."

And the gods continued to smile on me. A few days after I had started setting pins, I was sitting around the bowling alley waiting for someone, anyone, to start bowling when a man approached me. I could not believe my good fortune when he offered me a paper route. The route had twenty-six houses that took the Edmonton Journal, and I got a nickel a week for each house. I laughed and danced all the way home that night. Mom had been right; there was more to life than the stump farm.

And life was about to get better, much better. In January, Larry and I had landed a job peeling ties at the SNA lumber yard west of town. Saturdays and Sundays were the most profitable, because we got to work the whole day. Weekdays were a little tougher. After school we would both run home and change clothes, then as fast as our little legs would carry us we would run to the lumber yard. If we were real lucky, we could get ten or twelve ties peeled before I had to race away to the bowling alley to set pins. We weren't lucky enough to get to do the squares, which were normally bare of any bark, they were reserved for one of the owner's sons. We got the flats that had bark on two sides and required a considerable amount of effort to get the frozen bark off. For our efforts, we got five cents a tie. A whole nickel split two ways.

My routine was consistent, every weekday was the same. Get up in the morning and drag my butt to school. Then after school, race home, then race to the tie piles at the lumber yard, then race to the bowling alley. After that I would run to the Edson Hotel at the south end of town. There, I would meet the late night Greyhound Bus from Edmonton. I'd count out my papers with the other carriers, walk to my route and deliver the papers on the north end of town.

I could be at the bowling alley right now making a nickel a line, I thought as I limped onto the path in the vacant lot. My routine had come to a sudden smashing halt the previous night. The nickel-a-line, five-cent-paper and half-a-nickel tie bonanza had been side-tracked. However, I could thank my lucky stars that my ankle wasn't broken. I had been setting pins when one of the bowlers decided to throw an extra ball. Not knowing that there was incoming mail, I leapt off my perch just as the ball zoomed into the pit. It hit my ankle and flipped me like a top. As the world turned, my feet went skyward and I came down in the mess of balls and pins in the pit, right on my head.

Now, I was not racing to the SNA to peel ties, nor

was I setting pins. I was not even delivering papers. To drown my sorrows and ease my pain, I had limped my way to the movies. I was spending some of my hard-earned cash.

As I tromped along, alone in my misery, it dawned on me that I had walked every street, alley, sidewalk and vacant lot in Edson. For the first time in my life, I think I realized that I had never feared the creatures of the night or the supernatural, nor had I ever believed in aliens. I was not afraid of the dark. I chuckled as I boldly limped forward.

However, to every rule there is an exception. On this night, after moving about halfway across the vacant lot, I started to get this uncomfortable feeling. I looked over my shoulder, back towards the street. No, I was not just uncomfortable. I was pretty darned spooked, every muscle in my body was tense. I was ready for instant flight, I thought as the throbbing in my ankle increased.

As the fear of the unknown set in I found myself wishing I had never gone to the theatre. I could be in my own room right now in the safety and comfort of my home, in my own bed resting my ankle. But no, I am a man of adventure, so here I am in the middle of nowhere with visions of sinister things flashing through my mind.

I had slowly walked north on Main Street. I turned left on 5th Avenue, my normal route home, but after walking past the medical clinic and cutting through the back alley, I wished that I had not been so stupid. I wished I had gone straight up Main and turned on 7th.

It was just before midnight and I was having a devil of a time trying not to think about the movie I had just seen. Walking along Main Street with all its street and store lights I had not given the movie a second thought, but now I was experiencing a whole new sensation. It was something foreign to me. The movie had given me a whole new perspective on the perils of walking home, at night, in the dark. Walking in the darkness, I could see every imaginary creature, Martian or whatever, known to or conceived of by man. They were lurking behind every bush, every building; they were in every shadow.

I had watched the movie, spellbound, as those sneaky creatures had landed on earth, then burrowed into the ground and set their trap, waiting for an unsuspecting earthling to walk past. I was fascinated, as I sat and watched as an earthling approached the trap. Suddenly, the earth started to swirl, just a small spot unnoticeable at first, but it rapidly increased in speed and size, like an eddy in the river it whipped around, sucking everything down. In a swirl of sand and dirt the terrified earthling disappeared into the bowels of the earth. Into the trap. I watched as they inserted a pin in the back of the head, at the base of the spine. Then the human was returned to the surface where his actions were controlled by the Martians through the pin.

Having seen this movie and knowing what Martians were capable of, my imagination was in high gear; it was working overtime. For the first time in my life, there were other beings and suddenly they were something to fear. God alone knew that I was scared. I could just feel the Martians' presence. They were there for the sole purpose of snatching my body and whisking me away to outer space. I didn't know whether or not there was a cloud in the sky, a shooting star or a full moon. My eyes were busy searching the ground and darting in and out of the ominous shadows. I didn't have time to look up. I was not enjoying myself one little bit as I inched my way along.

I imagined they, the Martians, had burrowed into the ground and were there, hiding under sand. But there was no sand, only clay. Oh well, they were in the clay, too, they were waiting for me to pass by. I could imagine myself stepping on the ground where they had chosen to set their trap. In a flash they would be sucking me into the ground and taking control of my body.

When I reached the sidewalk on 6th I thanked God for getting me through the alley without falling into the trap. I would stay on the sidewalks as much as that was possible for the rest of the walk home. Here, I reasoned, the aliens could not suck me through the cement.

I spent a good week of my life during the next ten minutes or so that it took me to walk home and I would have loved to have run the last twenty feet from the sidewalk to the house. But that would be foolhardy, I reasoned, and besides my ankle wouldn't hold out. The last twenty feet just happened to be all dirt. It would be far more prudent to carefully pick my way to the front door and watch for any movement that would indicate a Martian trap. Slowly I crossed the lawn. With every step I could feel the earth swirling downward like a giant eddy pulling me in.

Finally, I was at the door, in the house. I was safe, I had beaten the Martian at his game.

I set about getting ready for bed. I told myself how

stupid I had been, that the fears that had dogged me all the way home were nothing more then an overactive imagination.

My bedroom was in the south-west corner of the house that my father was still in the process of building. In the sanctity of my own home I forgot about the movie, the Martians and the fear. I went to bed completely at ease. As I snuggled into my bed and turned out the lights, I could see out my window that the night was indeed very clear and the stars were shining brightly. I marvelled at their beauty.

A slight breeze blew up and the leaves on the poplar tree outside my window started to dance as the currents of air stroked them. Suddenly the tranquillity of the evening was shattered as my imagination once again took hold of me. I imagined all sorts of things were casting those dancing shadows over my window. My fear of the unknown was once again being drawn to the surface.

I lay there in the warmth and safety of my bed with my eyes glued to the windows, watching the shadows cast by the leaves as they thickened into a mass that I was sure was a Martian. Then as the leaves fluttered and the branches swayed, the dark mass would drift apart only to form another shadow that was larger and more ominous than the one before. This night, I felt, would be a long one. I doubted very much that I would sleep. Why did I ever go to that movie, I thought.

I lay there in misery, in the silence, waiting. Waiting for what? I had no idea.

"WHUMP!" It was a loud crashing sound. I knew I had felt the house shake. "Oh no, something just landed on our roof," I muttered aloud. When that thing, whatever it was, hit the roof, I hit the ceiling. My heart, which had been racing for most of the night, now started to pound like crazy in my ears. The sound was deafening. To say that I was scared at this point would be an understatement; I was petrified. My worst fears had been confirmed, there were Martians and they had just landed on our roof. On our house. They had come for me, I was sure of it.

I huddled down under the covers, pulling them right up to my chin. I needed all the protection I could get. I did not take my eyes off the window — they were glued to those perpetual dancing shadows. I knew that any moment now one of the Martians was going to fly through the window and grab me.

I was too scared to move, not knowing where the attack would come from. Maybe they would come down the chimney. Maybe they would bore a hole through the wall. Maybe they were going to take the whole house. They were awfully silent after they landed. Not a sound. Maybe they left, I thought. I hoped. I prayed.

Then I heard it, faintly at first, but I heard it. At the far side of the house, on the roof, somewhere over the living room, it was moving. I heard it as soon as it started. Then the noise got louder and I realized to my horror it was coming my way. Whatever it was, it was coming across the roof and it was coming for me. My number was up, of that I was certain.

I listened and did not move a muscle, except for my eyes, which were trained on the ceiling following the sound of the unknown across the roof. As I listened, the sound got louder. It was like a train building steam and picking up speed as it came towards my corner of the house. I could feel it gaining momentum. It was coming faster, faster, all the time gaining speed as the noise increased. It's my heart, I'll bet it can hear my heart beating. It picked up the sound and honed in on my heart. I held my breath, but that didn't work. My heart only sounded louder. I was doomed.

My eyes followed the noise as it came right over the top of me, like a roaring freight train. It passed right over my bed, over my body, my head and then suddenly it was deathly quiet. It had stopped. The sound had stopped. In the silence there were only the shadows of the leaves, dancing wildly on the windows. About that time, I thought my heart might have stopped, but the pounding told me it hadn't. I held my breath and waited. I prayed that whatever it was had left, had gone to prey on someone else. I could have given it a number of names that would have been far more suitable than me.

Suddenly, through the dancing leaves, a black torpedo-shaped object flashed across my window, speeding towards earth. My heart leapt right into my mouth.

BANG. CRASH. CRACK. SNAP. My heart skipped a few more beats, then proceeded to pound crazily again. I thought I was going to die, right there in my bed, when I saw that thing fly past my window and heard it crash outside.

Whatever it was had just landed in the pile of boards and scraps that had been thrown in a heap on the ground outside my window. The thing, the Martians, hadn't left. The brief pause and quiet had only been them leaving the roof before they landed on the ground. My eyes were wide open and I dared not move a muscle. Now I knew for sure every shadow that danced across the window pane was a Martian. They were toying with me, waiting for me to go to sleep so they could grab me. I knew I wouldn't be around to see the next day. I knew I was doomed.

As suddenly as the shadow sped earthward and the crash in the scrap pile had exploded outside my window, silence came. There was only the sound of the wind through the poplar tree, through the branches and the leaves. But the dancing shadows remained. They were the constant reminder that the Martians were just outside.

The next thing I knew, the sun was shining and it was a glorious day. I have no idea how long I laid there before sleep had come. I looked around the room in amazement. I was not inside a space ship full of Martians. I was in my bedroom, in my house.

That I was still lying in my bed in the morning was nothing short of a miracle. How did they miss me, I wondered, who did they get? Maybe they're still here. They could be outside waiting.

I got out of bed and limped my way to the window and slowly, very slowly, peered into a beautiful sunlit morning. The tree was still there, its branches and leaves hanging very still in the breathless light. I looked down at the ground not knowing what to expect. Everything looked pretty much the same as I remembered it. There was no space ship sitting in our backyard.

But what had hit our roof? That wasn't in the movie and surely I couldn't have just imagined something landing on the roof over the living room, then charging across the length of the house, passing right over my bedroom before crashing into the pile of scrap lumber on the ground beside my window. I remember, I saw its shadow as it plunged towards the earth. That was no dream.

I pushed forward for a better look and then noticed one thing that did not belong on the scrap pile.

Our house that Dad was still building was flat-roofed. Although he had sealed it, he had decided it would be better if he put on one more layer of rubberoid roofing and tar. He had left a number of rolls of roofing paper on the roof. One of them had obviously been left standing. The torpedo-shaped space ship I saw last night was a roll of rubberoid roofing that the wind had blown over. That was what had rolled across the flat surface, directly over my bedroom and then crashed into the scrap pile.

There it was, I could see it clearly, right in the middle of the scrap heap: one brand new roll of roofing. I knew all along that there weren't any such things as Martians, I told myself as I dressed.

Before leaving the bedroom, I snuck back to the window for one last look.

Out into the kitchen I limped. Mom and Dad were having a heated discussion about noises on the roof. Mom turned as I walked into the room.

"How does your ankle feel?" she asked.

"Pretty good," I replied, walking a little straighter.

"You look like you're just about ready to go back to work," Dad added.

"Uh. Well...I was thinking that maybe I should check around town for a day job," I answered, trying to get a better look at the back of their heads. After all, I thought, one can never be too careful.

THE JEEP TRAIL

After two months of pestering and begging for a job, my persistence was rewarded. I was sitting in the passenger's seat of a forestry green pick-up being driven by an old Forest Ranger with the Alberta Forest Service. We were heading south on the Coal Branch Highway, our destination the Leyland Ranger Station. After seeing my face at their counter every day for two months, I think the Alberta Forest Service was tired of me because they finally agreed to give me a job for the summer months, as far away from Edson as possible. I was heading south to work with the Forest Ranger from the Leyland district.

The highway in those days was gravel, dirt and a lot of dust. The road was winding and the drive took the better part of the day with the old ranger filling me in on all the points of interest, the history and even introducing me to some of the locals that we met along the way. The old ranger knew everybody, at least everybody that we stopped to see, and it seemed to me that we were stopping at every house between Edson and Leyland.

We drove for an eternity along the narrow highway through spruce and pine forests that in many places grew right up to the edge of the highway. Up and down long steep hills and mountainsides we travelled, our ears popping from the altitude changes. Each ear popping was accurately predicted by the old ranger. Finally, we left the spruce and pine forest and drove into the willow-covered lowlands along the McLeod River before entering the meadows in the beautiful mountain valley where the town of Cadomin and the Leyland Ranger Station are located.

Looking south along the valley I was immediately impressed with the mountains on both sides. They appeared to grow from the very town itself. "That's Cadomin Mountain to the left on the east side of town and Leyland Mountain to the right, on the west side of town," said the old ranger. He was a walking encyclopedia when it came to knowledge of the Coal Branch.

Through the pass at the south end of the valley you could see more mountains. Cadomin and Leyland were nestled in a valley surrounded by mountains. It was truly a magnificent scene and absolutely breathtaking. It was a good thing I was sitting in the old ranger's truck. If not, I probably would have got a darn good sunburn on the roof of my mouth from looking up. It was a spectacular sight.

"As soon as you get through the pass there to the south," the old ranger pointed to where the McLeod

River and the Whitehorse Creek came together, "the railroad and the highway follow the McLeod up to Mountain Park. Just before you cross the bridge on the Whitehorse, there's a trail to the right that will take you right into Jasper National Park. You'll get to see both before you leave this valley," he assured me.

"Cadomin's almost a ghost town now," said the old ranger sadly. "In June of '52 the McLeod flooded into the mine. It closed down in July. Most everybody moved away after that. There's not too many people left here anymore. You'll see a lot of empty houses with their doors and windows boarded up." His eyes turned misty and I thought the old ranger might cry as he remembered days long since passed.

The ranger station at Leyland was located on the north end of Cadomin and was a separate entity, like it sort of belonged to the town, but yet it didn't. It would be a good walk from the station into Cadomin, as I would soon find out on my weekly trek for groceries to the only store located on the far south end of town.

When one entered the forestry compound at Leyland, the first building encountered was the garage. It was sort of set off by itself and was separated from the rest of the buildings by the railroad. A walk from the bunkhouse to the garage and back again meant that a person had to cross the railroad tracks twice. I looked at this building when we drove by and noticed the large beams protruding on the north side. I had never seen anything like them in my life. They came from the top of the wall and angled back to the ground sort of like a large brace. It looked to me like someone was going to add onto the building and after getting the beams set up on one side and attached to the building, they had a change of mind and just let the other ends fall to the ground and there they stayed.

"Did someone get tired of building or forget to build the back wall where those beams have fallen?" I asked.

"No, no," replied the old ranger. He sounded just a little amused at my less-than-knowledgeable question. "Those are braces to keep the building from blowing away."

"Oh yeah, I'll bet," I replied. "You can't fool me on that one."

"Oh, I'm serious. The wind really blows up here," the old ranger said. "You remember the pass to the south, past the town? You know, the one I showed you when we were driving in."

"Yeah, I can see the pass all right, but you can't fool me about the wind blowing this garage away. I wasn't born yesterday." I may have been just a kid at the time, but there was no way the old ranger was going to get me to believe a story like that. I knew that if I fell for that story I would be the laughingstock of the Forest Service and a prize candidate for many more sucker stories.

"Believe me, young fella," snorted the old ranger indignantly. "I'm telling you the truth. The wind up here blows so hard that most of the houses are braced to keep them from blowing away. Even then when the wind really blows, roofs have been blown right off many of the houses in town."

"Sure, sure," I chuckled. "Next you'll tell me it's just like the big bad wolf."

"Come on, let's go over to the ranger station and the

bunkhouse and you'll see, they're all braced up, too," the old ranger snapped. "The problem with you kids today is you're too damn smart for your own good. You think you know it all. I'll have you know I was the ranger up here for several years. I've seen many roofs blown off. In fact, I've seen entire houses that were blown away."

"Oh yeah, sure," I replied.

"Follow me," commanded the old ranger and we proceeded over to the ranger station and the bunkhouse. He stomped along like a man on a mission. I followed behind and sure enough both of these buildings had the same type of bracing on the north side and they were anchored solidly in the ground. "Well, young man, what do you think of that?" he challenged.

Not wanting to concede anything at this point I said, "Well, maybe forestry does that with their buildings, but I'll bet they don't do that in town."

"Okay," snorted the old ranger. "If that's the way you want it then, get back into the truck, we're going into town." The old ranger didn't say much on the short drive in, but the set of his jaw told me that he meant business. There were not many streets in Cadomin, but we drove up and down each and every one. Some of the houses did indeed have similar braces lodged on the north side of the building and firmly imbedded in the ground. The old ranger was kind enough to point a finger at each and every one without uttering a single word.

I didn't say much more as we returned to the ranger station to meet the district ranger.

My home for the next two months was to be the bunkhouse which I would share with one other person. He wasn't there when I arrived, but it was obvious that he was not too far away and that he had already staked claim to one of the two cots. The bunkhouse was a one-room cabin, containing two single cots, one small stove, a table, two chairs and a small washstand. Later that evening I met my roommate.

"Can you cook?" he asked me. It was his way of saying hello.

"Nope," I replied.

"Well," he said, "since I was here first, I'll cook 'til you complain. Then you take over the cooking 'til I complain and we'll change back and forth each time the other guy complains. How's that sound?"

"Sounds good to me," I said.

Secretly I was patting myself on the back for getting out of that one. When I said I couldn't cook, boy, I meant it. Mom had always done all the cooking at home and I never had to worry about it. As luck would have it, I still wasn't going to have to worry about it.

Next morning bright and early my roommate was up and cooking breakfast. Man, I loved the smell of coffee and pancakes in the morning, especially since I was able to stay in bed. Reluctantly, I dragged my butt out of bed, washed and sat down at the table. I complimented my roomy for the great spread and dug in. Those pancakes tasted as good as they smelled and man did he ever cook up a stack of them. Now, I'm a big eater, but even I couldn't eat all of the pancakes he had already stacked on the plate, and still he cooked more. My roomy was a pancake-cookin' fool.

Hey, I thought when we broke for lunch, what a great idea! Pancakes for lunch. My roomy set out a spread of cold pancakes with a can of peanut butter. We had both been working outside on separate projects and didn't really have time to return to the bunk house and cook up a hot lunch. Cold pancakes were just fine. No complaints here.

Man, this is ridiculous, I thought, looking at the supper table and the stack of cold pancakes. What gives anyway, this had to be some kind of sick joke. We were back at the bunkhouse in plenty of time for my roomy to prepare a nice hot supper. But here I was, staring at a stack of cold pancakes with a side order of pork and beans, cold pork and beans, for supper. I figured when a man worked his butt off all day he deserved better, but what the heck, I'd had worse and things would only get better when my roomy realized that I wasn't a whiner. That's right, no complaints from my corner. I smiled at my roomy as I dug into the cold offerings.

Next morning I again awoke to the smell of hot coffee and pancakes, they smelled and tasted just as good as they had yesterday morning. I looked at my roomy slaving over the stove. Just look at him, I moaned to myself, he's cooking another stack of pancakes that would choke an ox. I knew before I finished breakfast the meals today would be the same as yesterday. I had no delusions; this pattern would continue for the next two months. I could only pray that every second week I would get a reprieve. My folks had promised to come to Leyland every second Friday night and take me home for the weekend. There, I would get my clothes washed and — heaven forbid — have a decent meal. In fact, I would get several decent meals. Anything other than pancakes would be a treat.

When I would talk to the ranger in charge, he would tell me that when a person got on a fire crew, fighting a forest fire, you got fed real good meals. After a week of my roomy's cooking, I was praying for a forest fire. By the end of the summer I was ready to go out and set a fire myself, but the way my luck was running they probably would have brought in a cook that only knew how to make pancakes. As my roomy cooked and I ate, I often gagged thinking that I was destined to eat pancakes for the rest of my life.

My first morning on the job. I was rarin' to go. I was going to be working with Curly and would be doing all of the neat things that a Forest Ranger did. I always wondered what it was that they did. I would see their forestry green trucks go roaring up and down the road, but never did really know where they went. They certainly did a lot of driving, but the other tasks they performed remained a mystery. I was full of anticipation at the thought of the unknown and just chomping at the bit to get started.

"I suppose we had better find something for you to do," said Curly, standing there looking at me. "I'm not even sure why they sent you here. I didn't ask for you and don't really need you up here." He looked at me accusingly.

"I'm gonna be a Forest Ranger," I replied, staring at this guy who obviously didn't want me. Why would he be called Curly, I wondered, when his straight dark hair is cut so short. "I'm supposed to go with you and learn what a Forest Ranger does. That's for when I get my own district," I blurted out. "I'm gonna be a Forest Ranger when I finish school."

I could see what was gonna happen here in a real hurry if I couldn't convince Curly that I was to be like an assistant ranger. I was going to get stuck with some lousy job or worse yet, sent home. A lousy job would be bad enough, but being sent home meant no job at all and no job meant no money. Jobs and money were both hard to come by in Edson.

"Okay," Curly sighed. "So you want to do what a Forest Ranger does, eh? Come on out to the garage then and we'll get started."

Ha, I thought, I survived this one and off we went to the garage, Curly leading and me following.

"Grab that shovel, that pick and that empty Spork® can," Curly directed.

"What do I need the empty Spork® can for?" I asked, picking up the pick and shovel then eyeing the empty can, thinking that I should just leave it there.

"You'll see. Come on out here with me and we'll get started."

I noticed that I was the only one carrying any tools as we walked out and Curly advised that we were going to put a fence around the east side of the garage so that equipment could be safely stored.

Curly had a long length of rope and the two of us set about staking out the area to be fenced off. It was just as I had imagined, my dreams come true. Here I was working with the ranger building a fence. I wasn't sure if this was all they did, but at least I was working with him, sort of like an assistant.

After measuring the area and putting a little stake in

the exact spot where Curly wanted each post, I was advised that the posts had to be set three to four feet in the ground.

"The closer to four feet the better, so the frost doesn't push them out of the ground," Curly said. "You can always tell when posts aren't in deep enough and the frost is pushing them up because they start to lean from side to side and look like hell. They have to be set deep enough, now remember that. They also have to be straight in line with each other. I don't want to see a line of posts that a snake would break his back on if he tried to crawl along it."

Curly stood back, admiring his work and eyeing the line of stakes, sort of making a few mental notes before he indicated that he was satisfied with everything.

"You'll find the digging here a bit tough," Curly advised. "But you have everything you need to dig the holes. Don't forget, three to four feet deep and keep them in a straight line or you'll be pulling them out and redoing them. You understand?"

I indicated that I did and wondered why he was making such a big fuss over it since we were working together.

"I'll be back later to check on you." With that Curly did what I was used to seeing Forest Rangers do, he got into his forestry green truck and roared off down the road. At that point I had a pretty good idea what the assistant did, but I still had no idea what the ranger did.

Three to four feet down, posts in a straight line, why that shouldn't be too hard to do, I thought to myself. I picked up the shovel and prepared to dig where the first stake was located. I placed the shovel at the appropriate spot and angle and placed my foot on the top of it to push it into the ground. I was no stranger to shovels, they had been a big part of our life on the stump farm. I had dug lots of holes in the clay and muskeg. This would be a snap. I knew it wouldn't be long before I was sitting with Curly in the passenger's seat of his forestry green truck. I could just picture myself roarin' down the road with the window open and the wind blowing in my face.

I pushed my foot down on the shovel to drive it into the earth. What the devil, the shovel didn't go into the ground here like it did at home. In fact it didn't go in at all. I replaced it and jammed my foot harder against the blade only to have the handle twist in my hand as the blade slid along the side of a rock.

I stepped back and reassessed the situation, then grabbed for the pick. The ground here was all gravel and I figured probably just packed hard from being driven on. I knew how to fix that, a couple of whacks with the pick would loosen it and then I could scoop it out with the shovel. No sweat there.

Hoisting the pick over my head I plunged it towards the ground, just like ringing the bell at the circus, I said to myself as I gave it all I had. I knew a good shot would loosen a bunch of rocks and gravel all at once. The point of the pick plunged swiftly into the ground, right on target. There was a sharp report of metal hitting solid rock and the pick went crazy. The point of the pick spun to the right side, causing the handle to twist violently in my hands. But I had a good grip on that handle; I didn't give in easily, which resulted in blisters on both hands as the pick handle tore free. My hands were stinging and my arms and shoulders were vibrating from the ground's unexpected rejection of the pick head. Geez, I said to myself, what happened? I peered down at the little mark on the ground where the pick had entered. There was a larger gouge to the side where the pick had exited and thrown about a handful of gravel across the lot. Scraping away the loose gravel I found a very large boulder which I had hit almost dead-center with the pick. Man, it was right where I had to dig that damn post hole.

It was time to reassess just what had to happen here in order to get the hole dug. I looked at the shovel and knew that I couldn't get it into the ground, let alone move that boulder. The pick could be used, but it wasn't going to be forced to do anything when it encountered rock. I was beginning to get a pretty good idea of the value of the Spork® can in digging fence post holes at the ranger station in Leyland.

I tried to use the shovel to scrape away whatever loose rock and gravel it could reach. It worked sometimes, but was slow and awkward. More often then not the wide spoon-shaped blade was too large to be of much good.

The pick was used to dislodge some of the more stubborn compacted sand and gravel in the hole and it also acted as a pretty good lever for dislodging some of the smaller rocks. It had its limits as a lever, though, and I sure as hell didn't want to break the handle on that boulder.

I looked at that damn Spork® can and started to cuss it. This was going to be a lot harder and slower than I thought. I picked up the can and got down on all fours.

It was the Spork® can that I used to dig those holes and we got to know each other pretty good over the next couple of weeks.

The Spork® can was quicker and more effective than the shovel in scraping away loose rock and sand as it would fit into smaller places. When large rocks were encountered the Spork® can was the only tool that could be used to scrape and scratch away the sand and gravel until the rock could be dislodged and removed. Needless to say, the Spork® can became the most useful tool and those fence post holes were dug with me spending most of the time on my hands and knees or sprawled on my belly.

The last inch of those three to four-foot-deep holes was dug with my arm stretched to its full length down the hole, praying that the top didn't cave in before the hole was completed. Normally the top of the hole opening for a fence post is six inches. These hummers were often three feet across depending on the size of the rock encountered. Some of those bloody holes took a half a day to dig and looked more like a crater than a post hole.

It wasn't long before I was cursing forestry, gravel, shovels, picks, fence posts and that damn Spork® can. And every morning, noon and night I had a stack of pancakes to look forward to. Come on, forest fire, I prayed, where the hell are you when you're needed.

Finally, the fence was finished. Each post was three to four feet in the ground and they were all in a straight line. The last of the craters had been filled in. Curly was pleased, at least I think he was. He did sorta nod his head as if to say it was a good job.

Now we were going to do some real rangering. Curly and I had loaded a large tent into the back of the forestry green pick-up along with a week's supply of groceries, a stove, a couple of plates and utensils, our sleeping bags and fishing poles and we were off, roarin' down the road. Just driving down the highway, we were doing real ranger type work.

"We're going to be cutting a trail from the highway into the MacKenzie Creek Falls," Curly informed me. "We take off up the MacKenzie Creek, just upstream from the bridge across the McLeod River."

"Isn't there a trail there now?" I asked.

"Oh yeah, but it's just a hiking trail. You can't get a jeep down it," Curly replied.

"Why do you need to get a jeep down it?" I asked.

"You never know when you're going to need a jeep in that country," Curly stated. "It's pretty rough and rugged in there. A lot of people come in here to fish and hunt. We need the road in case there's a forest fire. Then you need quick access or it can get away from you pretty quick."

"So we're actually going to be building a road? And just how are we going to build this road?" I inquired, remembering the fence.

"Oh, I brought along some tools for that. Don't worry, I'll show you how to use them," he chuckled.

Yeah, I thought to myself, remembering the Spork® can, I'll bet you will. Since Curly didn't help with the fence, I was sure that he would be just as helpful building the road, especially if it had to be dug with a Spork® can. I could picture myself building the road while Curly fished. Yeah, that would be my luck.

The trail up the MacKenzie Creek was not that far out of Leyland, I thought. It was close enough to drive out every day, until I remembered the pancakes.

"Can you cook?" I asked Curly.

"Sure can," he replied. "I'm a good camp cook. How about you?"

"Naw. I'm not very good. I never learned how."

"Looks like I cook then and you do the bull cooking," he replied with a grin.

Suddenly I thought that camping sounded far better then returning to Leyland every night. Curly could cook. Things were definitely looking up as Curly pulled the truck off the highway and we proceeded to unload. Man, we had a lot of supplies, I thought as I looked at the growing mound. But I couldn't help myself, I started to whistle happily as I thought about it, Curly could cook.

"How we gonna get all of these supplies into the falls?" I asked.

Curly just grinned and said, "You said you wanted to be a Forest Ranger, didn't you?"

"Yeah," I replied.

"Well young ranger-to-be, one of the first things you learn is that being a Forest Ranger means you get to pack your supplies. You and me, we're going to pack them in, on our backs."

"You gotta be kiddin," I replied. "That'll take us all week."

"Not so," said Curly. "We'll do it in one trip. We're going to divide up the load and tie it onto these two pack boards. That's no problem, it'll work, you'll see."

Curly was right, we divided up the gear and packed it onto the pack boards.

"Each man carries his own gear," Curly informed me as we started to divide the load. "You take your sleeping bag and half of the groceries, I take my bag and half the groceries. I'll take the dishes and the cutlery. There's two pulaski tools, a shovel and a swede saw. I'll take one pulaski tool and the shovel, you get the other pulaski and the saw. Oh yeah," he chuckled, "did I forget to mention, you get the tent. Give me a hand and we'll get it onto your pack."

The tent was an old canvas heavyweight about 10 feet by 14 feet. It looked like it was older than both Curly and myself and with all the dirt and grime rubbed into it I was sure that it probably weighed as much. When we grabbed it to pull it to the back of the truck, I knew that Curly must be joking about me carrying that bloody thing. It weighed a ton.

"Bullshit!" I said. "One man can't carry that bloody heavy tent on his back. Let alone the tent, a sleeping bag, and a week's groceries."

"Oh yeah, you can do it," said Curly. "Once you get everything properly lashed on and the pack centered on your back it'll be easy. You'll see."

With that Curly proceeded to show me how to pack a pack board. First thing on was the tent. It took both of us to lift it and center it on the pack board which we had placed on the tailgate of the truck.

"It has to be lashed on tightly so that it won't move when you walk," Curly advised. He sounded very serious, almost like a teacher trying to convince a very sceptical class.

When the tent was secured to Curly's satisfaction, he packed my half of the groceries into a sack and tied them onto my pack, above the tent. At the very top of the pack board went my sleeping bag. I had to admit, Curly was a master at getting all that stuff on those two pack boards, but I thought mine had a tad more on it then Curly's did.

Once we had both pack boards securely packed, mine was still on the tailgate, Curly helped me stand it up and get my arms through the shoulder straps. Well, that part wasn't too bad, I thought, but quickly changed my mind when I tried to stand up. The weight of the tent snapped my shoulders straight back as soon as the straps became taught. Think again, said my legs as they started to bow under the weight being thrust upon them. Whump, my butt hit the tailgate. I struggled to maintain my balance and I damn near ended up laying on top of the groceries, tent and pack board in the box of the damn forestry green truck.

"No way," I said to Curly. "I can't even stand with all this crap on my back, let alone walk."

"Don't worry, you're okay," Curly said encouragingly. "Give me your hand and I'll help you get to your feet. You just have to get used to carrying a pack. Once you've done it a few times you'll see how easy it is."

Look at this, I thought, who said Curly wouldn't help when you needed a hand? Here I was loaded like a pack mule and Curly was right there to offer his hand to get me to my feet. This was going to be a great trip with all the help that Curly was giving me. We were a team, me and Curly, rangering together.

"Now when you get to your feet, lean forward slightly," Curly instructed. "That way you'll be able to balance the load and walk with no difficulty at all. It's okay. You'll see."

This time I did not try to get up as quickly as I did the first time. Before trying to stand, I slowly leaned forward, feeling the weight of the tent, the sleeping bag and the groceries on my shoulders. With Curly's words of encouragement I leaned a little farther forward. The backpack sort of wanted to stay where it was and I felt this strange sensation in my shoulders, like they were going to be separated from my body. With me leaning forward straining at the load and Curly pulling, the weight suddenly shifted and came over my shoulders, forcing my whole body forward. I knew instantly that I was leaving the tailgate and that I had better get my feet under me, moving and damn fast. Nothing was going to stop that tent. I had to get mobile to keep that tent in the air. If I didn't the only place for it was on top of me. "For Pete's sake, legs, get moving," my face yelled. "If you don't that damn tent is going to drive me into the gravel." I could almost feel the rocks and sand being ground into my face. If I had fallen, the tent would have driven my head into the gravel like a fence post.

Curly was no fool. As soon as the leverage shifted and I started forward, he got the hell out of the way and started to yell for me to find a comfortable stance for balancing the load.

"Stand up a little straighter," shouted Curly. "No. No, not that much, lean forward a little more, that's too much, stand a little straighter. Don't lean to the side or you'll go over that way. Steady now, steady."

During all Curly's shouting of encouragement, I was leaning forward and racing straight ahead, aided by the tent. With Curly's timely instructions I tried to stand a little straighter. That was like applying the brakes and it was a good thing that Curly was there. He immediately recognized my error and was quick to direct me to lean forward again. If I had ever got backpedaling with that load I would have ended up back in Leyland and Curly wouldn't have had a tent to sleep in. This time I did not lean too far forward, but was still going in that direction when I stepped on a small rock. My foot slipped and my body immediately started to go sideways. My load was quick to follow.

Once again Curly came to my rescue when he yelled, "Don't lean to the side, stand up straight and keep moving forward." What would I have done without Curly's help, I thought. Curly was certainly a man you wanted on your side if you were in trouble. After dancing around for several minutes that seemed like hours, I finally found a stance where the pack would ride. I had to lean forward, that was good advice from Curly, it insured that I was always moving as the pack continually propelled me onward.

"Don't worry. You're going to be fine now, looks like you've got everything under control," Curly said in a very comforting tone. As I headed for the trail, Curly called out, "Not so fast there, young feller. We don't want you to forget your tools now, do we?"

"Right," I replied and I took a wide turn on the gravel and returned to the rear of the truck. Oh yes,

Curly had noted that both my hands were empty, but not for long as he retrieved the pulaski and the saw from the truck bed. He handed them to me as I motored by on legs that felt like Hiawatha's Bow as they strained and bent under their load.

"You're going to need these," he said. "Can't build a road without the proper tools."

At this point I was wondering where he had hidden the Spork® can. I knew that it had to be on my pack somewhere because Curly couldn't fit it on his load, not with the extra burden of the plates and utensils he was carrying.

With Curly leading the way we headed east, up the MacKenzie Creek towards the falls. Curly was right, the trail was only for hiking, you couldn't drive a jeep anywhere on it. What Curly had not mentioned was that you couldn't just walk down the path either. There were fallen trees all the way along and across it. They had to be climbed over. I would have loved to have crawled under some, but the size and weight of the pack wouldn't allow it. I knew if I ever got down on my hands and knees to crawl under I would never get up again. After about the first ten steps I took with that pack on, just the thought of getting down and not having to get up again sounded pretty good.

Now Curly was right about a lot of things, but he was dead wrong about that pack. It was centered on my back, but it sure as hell wasn't fine. If I slipped or misstepped just a little, which I did fairly often, I would have to grab or clutch at anything handy and I had to be very careful not to drop either the saw or the pulaski. Curly had already helped me so much that I didn't want to impose on him anymore by asking him to retrieve one of my tools.

I learned very quickly that there were only two ways that I dared to stop. One was to wrap my arms around the nearest tree, hang on and pray they didn't get pulled out of their sockets. The other was to locate a level spot beside a tree, lean back to slow down as I approached the spot, then quickly turn around and pray the pack came to rest against the tree. The second was the preferred way, but there were not too many level spots. Anyway, I didn't have much time to stop as I had to keep up with Curly.

Obstacles were everywhere on the trail. If it wasn't the deadfall across the path it was an outcropping of rock that I had to try to shinny around. Some of them proved to be difficult, almost impassable, but I was assured by Curly's encouraging words that I could do it. It occurred to me that for all his help and encouragement, not once did Curly offer to trade packs.

"Just a little farther. It's not as bad as it looks. You're doing fine. I told you it wasn't that bad. We'll be there any minute now," Curly reassured me continually.

Curly sure was a big help. I was going to learn a lot about being a ranger from him. So far I had learned how to dig a hole with a Spork® can and now I was getting firsthand experience on being a mule. I was learning how to carry a tent through the bush, alongside of a creek, over deadfall and around rock outcroppings. This was a wealth of knowledge that would stand me in good stead with future career decisions.

Whoa now, what is this, I wondered as I slammed into a tree to halt my forward progress. There was

Curly standing in the middle of the creek, in swiftly running water up to his knees and with a big shit-eating grin on his face.

"Are we there?" I yelled with great anticipation. We had to be there. Why else would Curly be standing in the middle of the damn creek?

"Nope," Curly said. "We have to ford her here. There's a rock slide up ahead and we can't get past it so we wade across."

Curly hadn't mentioned this and I sort of wondered out loud, "I wonder when that happened?"

"Oh that slide, it's been there all along, at least as long as I've been here. We have to ford the creek a couple of times before we get to the falls," Curly responded.

The bottom of the creek was solid rocks, none smaller than a softball and all slippery as hell. The water was rushing past pretty fast and it was up to Curly's knees. It didn't look too whiz bangy to me. Cripes, I'm having trouble standing on level ground. I've stumbled, clutched and grabbed my way so far and now he expects me to cross the damn creek.

"You gonna give me a hand gettin' across?" I asked hopefully.

"Don't worry, you'll be okay," Curly assured me, smiling again. "Oh and don't forget, if you fall in you have to sleep in a wet sleeping bag tonight. Good luck!"

That's just like Curly, I thought, what a guy, always concerned about my welfare.

With that the ranger was off again leading the way to the falls and the assistant was bringing up the rear. Dragging his ass would be a better description. I don't think I could have fallen at that point because I'm sure my butt was dragging on the ground. If it wasn't it sure felt like it.

Damn that water was cold and the rocks were more slippery than they looked. I had a hell of a time inching my way across that stream. I had to make sure that my foot was firmly planted before I took the next step. If I slipped there was nothing to grab onto. But there was no stopping, no hesitation, the tent continually urged me on.

Man, I wished to hell that I was back digging post holes. That little Spork® can was looking awfully good about now.

Eventually, I could hear the roar of the falls. They grew louder as I got closer and finally saw the site that Curly had chosen to set up camp. I was so tired when I got there I didn't think that I could even get the pack off of my back. True to form Curly didn't come over to help. I found a fairly smooth tree and backed up to it until the pack was resting on it, then I slowly lowered myself to the ground and slid out of the pack.

"Let's set the tent right over here on this high ground near the creek," directed Curly. "I'm going to go and catch us a fish for dinner."

Curly, fresh after a nice healthy walk, was off to the falls to do a little fishing and I was left to drag my butt around trying to set up the tent. My arms, legs and shoulders felt like hell and didn't want to work properly. I was sure that my shoulders had been dislocated. My back hurt, oh mother, I moaned, I ached all over. What a horrible experience that was. I was already hoping that we would get the road built so we could haul all that stuff out with the jeep. I didn't need another one of Curly's "easy, no problem" jobs.

Thank heaven this was an established camp ground and there were tent poles leaning against a tree. At least I didn't have to cut, limb and carry new ones. The old poles were also nice and dry and were well worn. The ridge pole slipped easily through the holes along the inside at the top of the tent and out the other end. Now it was just a matter of hoisting the ridge pole up and onto the cross poles at each end of the tent. Up she goes, I said to myself as I lifted the first end. Holy mackerel, I've got aches where I didn't even know that I had muscles. This little task would not normally have been a very big deal, but that damn tent had just about killed me. Would I ever get back to normal?

"I've got supper," yodelled Curly.

Big deal, I mumbled to myself as I watched him waltz back into camp with four nice rainbow trout hanging from a willow stringer. "How's the camp shaping up?"

"Just fine," I grumbled. "I'm going to cut some spruce boughs and make myself a bed before it gets dark. I want something nice and soft to sleep on tonight."

"You got the fire goin' yet?"

"In a minute," I mumbled. "In a minute." The fire could wait, I thought. I picked up the pulaski tool and headed for a nice stand of spruce trees. I knocked off about 75 bushy branches that were about 18 inches long. For a spruce bough bed you want thin branches that are very heavily covered with smaller branches and needles. These I carried back to the tent and after coming to an agreement with Curly over who slept where, I proceeded to build my bed.

Beginning where I wanted my head, I started laying out the spruce boughs one at a time. I spread them the width of my sleeping bag and then worked slowly down towards the bottom of the bed. Spruce bough beds are excellent mattresses, they keep you off the hard rocky ground and also dry, should there be any moisture in the soil.

Let Curly build his own bed. After all it was Curly who said, "Each man looks after his own bed roll."

While I was getting my bed area set up, Curly was busy waiting for the fire so that he could cook the trout for supper. How about that, fish for supper, no pancakes, I muttered as I admired the fine bed. Maybe I'll just lay down on my bed and relax for a minute before I start the fire, I said to myself as I lowered my pain-riddled body onto the spruce bough bed. Man, what a soft comfy bed. It's just like floating on a cloud. Laying on those spruce boughs was enough to make me forget the many aches and pains that wracked my tired body.

What's that? I opened my eyes slowly and looked around. A useless gesture for it was blacker than the inside of a cow and I couldn't see a thing. Where am I, I thought, forgetting about the previous day's experience. Did someone call? Am I dreaming or did someone call my name, I thought to myself as I lay very still, not moving. I stared around at the black void on the inside of the tent, still not sure of my bearings. Everything seemed to be a little fuzzy for some reason. I could feel the cold air of a mountain morning in my nostrils and hear the roar of the waterfall in the distance. Whatever it was, it did not register. Man, it felt so good just to lay there not moving. It's still early, lots of time for some more ZZZs, I thought and closed my eyes.

"Better get that fire going if you want breakfast before you hit the trail," Curly bellowed.

Now that I heard and I woke with a start. I wasn't used to someone bellowing that early in the morning. My eyes popped open and my head shot up as instant fright seized me. Wrong move. Fright wasn't the only thing that seized me. I knew it immediately, the pain that shot between my shoulder blades was like someone running a hot poker down my spine. I fell back to my bed and moaned. Now I was wide awake and the sudden movement, well actually any movement, was causing me all sorts of grief as the searing pain danced from one muscle to the other and back again. Oh man, I ached all over.

As I lay back on the bed trying not to move I became aware of the fact that I had all my clothes on. As a matter of fact, I was laying on the spruce boughs with my sleeping bag covering me like a blanket. My buddy Curly must have taken pity on me and covered me before hitting the sack himself. What a partner.

Curly had certainly got my attention with his early morning bellow that snapped me from my death-like sleep. "What happened to supper?" I asked, trying not to move and to postpone the inevitable.

"I ate it last night. There's nothing quite like a feed of fresh trout when you're on the trail. Too bad you fell asleep, you'd have enjoyed them," Curly replied. "But that's in the past, that was yesterday and this is today, it's time to get up now. Better get the fire going so I can cook us some breakfast. Up you get, you know the rules. The bull cook gets the fire going and does the dishes. Which reminds me, not only didn't you start the fire last night, but you didn't do dishes. So they have to be done this morning."

"What happened to my fish?" I asked.

"I told you I ate them, now let's get going," Curly responded, sounding a little irritated.

"Since I didn't eat any fish, I didn't dirty any dishes, so I guess I don't have to wash any," I said quite emphatically.

"I guess you just don't understand, son. When you're the bull cook, and you are the bull cook on this trip, you light the fire and do the dishes. I don't care if you don't eat for the whole trip. Get the picture?" Curly was much more emphatic than I was.

"Gotcha," I said. Curly sure had a way with words and I recognized the no-nonsense tone in his voice. I tried to throw off the sleeping bag, but my arm and shoulder said, "slow down boy, things ain't working quite up to snuff here this morning." I almost made it, but decided that it might be easier to crawl out from under it instead. Crawling was more painful than throwing. Now my whole body rebelled. If I hadn't hurt so bad I would have screamed. I wasn't having much luck trying to sit up either, nothing was working right. Maybe if I roll over, I thought and slowly pushed myself over on my side and succeeded in rolling off the spruce boughs. There was more searing pain as I lay on my stomach on the hard cold ground. I worked my way up until I was on my hands and knees. Every bone, every muscle in my body screamed defiance at me.

"Oh man, does my body ache now," I moaned. Luckily I fell asleep with all my clothes on. I don't think I could have bent down to pull my pants on, let alone tie my shoes.

As I stumbled to my feet and groped around in the dark I had a horrible thought. I didn't prepare any kindling for the morning fire. Maybe Curly did.

"Did you by chance cut any kindling for the fire this morning?" I asked Curly in a pleading, weak voice.

"Nope. That's the bull cook's job," Curly replied from the warmth and comfort of his sleeping bag.

"Thanks loads," I said and fell through the flap on the tent.

It wasn't much brighter outside the tent than it was on the inside and it was a whole lot damper as everything was covered with a heavy dew. Lovely, just lovely I muttered as I groped around under the spruce trees trying to find some dry dead twigs that I could use to start a fire with. There were lots of twigs, but not many dry ones. I'd have to remember not to make that mistake again. From now on there would be feather sticks, dry twigs and wood in the tent.

Thank the good lord for the dry paper on the inside of the tent, otherwise I never would have got that damp wood to burn. Soon Curly was busy cooking breakfast. Bacon and eggs. Man, did they smell good. I was hungry as a horse, in fact I think I could have eaten the arse out of a skunk I was so hungry.

Better wash up before breakfast, I thought and headed for the creek and splashed water on my face.

Whoa! Now that's cold, what a way to wake up in the morning. Boy, my body didn't need that shock on top of the aches and pains. From now on it's heated water, enough of this outdoorsy mountain man crap for me.

Back at the tent Curly advised me, "You haven't done last night's dishes yet, young fella. Better get crackin' or there won't be anything to put the breakfast on."

Back to the creek I went with the canvas bucket and got a bucketful of water. Wash the dishes. Eat breakfast. Wash the dishes.

"Let's go to work," said Curly.

"You sure take all the fun out of camping," I griped at Curly.

"This, my fine young friend, is not a camping trip," responded Curly. "This is a working trip and you are about to find that out. Now grab the saw and a pulaski tool and let's get going. No more bellyaching. Follow me."

With that we started down the trail. But not very far. At the first windfall we stopped and Curly directed what had to be done and how we would do it.

"Each windfall has to be removed from the trail," Curly directed, "and remember there has to be enough room to get a jeep through, so we have to cut an opening at least eight feet wide. You can remove most of the windfalls by making only two cuts, but some of the larger ones will have to be cut several times. Cut this one here and again back here and then throw the cut portion back off the trail."

"Okay," I replied. "We going to do this all the way back to the highway?" I asked as I began to saw.

"That's right," said Curly as he carefully watched how I handled his saw.

"Wouldn't it have made more sense to have started at the other end, coming out from the station every morning?" I asked, thinking that the pancakes may not have been so bad after all. "That way we wouldn't have had to climb over all of this stuff with those heavy packs."

"Wouldn't have been the same," said Curly. "You appreciate what you're doing more this way, and besides we wouldn't have the opportunity to camp out as much."

"I'm sure I would have enjoyed it quite a bit more," I said, throwing the cut-off portion of the tree to one side while my muscles kept yelling at me to take it easy.

"Looks wide enough to me," said Curly, surveying the opening left when the first windfall was removed. "Lets go, there's plenty more."

"Yeah, I know, I climbed over every one of them. Me and the tent, we know them all personally," I responded sarcastically.

With the pulaski tool we chopped and hoed small roots, stumps and rocks off of the trail.

"I think you've got this mastered," Curly said after we had removed several deadfalls and about a truck load of roots, stumps and rocks. "Let's go on down to the creek and work on the first crossing."

At the first crossing Curly carefully surveyed the entire area before making a decision. "We'll build the bridge here at this narrow point in the creek," Curly said. "It means we'll have to remove a little timber and change the trail a bit, but it's a better place for a bridge.

We're going to need two real good timbers that will be used for the beams. Then we'll cut some cross-braces. Don't forget the cross-braces have to be eight feet long so that we can get a jeep across. They should all be about the same size, five to six inches in width. The beams will have to be dug in on both sides and they'll have to be dug deep enough so that the cross beams come level to the ground. Don't want to damage the jeep by making it jump up onto the bridge, now do we?"

For some reason Curly was sure giving me a lot of "don't forgets" even though we were working as a team.

With those instructions firmly implanted in my head, Curly and I set out to clear the area. We used the saw to cut the timbers and the pulaski tool for everything else. I began to appreciate just what a good useful tool the pulaski was. Once the sites on both sides of the creek were cleared it was time to get the beam timbers cut. That was another experience. At home I had old Barney, my logging horse, to drag any trees that needed moving, but out here it was just Curly and me. Curly gave me a lot of encouragement during this phase of the bridge building. Although I was still stiff and sore, my muscles had stopped screaming at me.

There was sure a lot of grunting and groaning once those trees were on the ground. We pulled them, we pushed them, we pried them, we did everything imaginable until we got them to where Curly was happy with them. Then we started to cut the cross-braces. These were not nearly as heavy, they were about half the length and quite a bit smaller.

"Cross-braces have to be notched a little where they lay on the beam," Curly explained as he showed me how to properly notch each cross-brace and fit it onto the beam. "Don't lay all the big ends of the braces on the same side, always alternate them. It makes for a better ride when you have to cross with the jeep. We'll bring in drift pins on the next trip to nail them down. That'll make a nice sturdy safe bridge."

"What's a drift pin?" I asked.

"It's like a long spike that you use to nail down timbers," explained Curly. "There's a bunch of them back at the ranger station. You can bring them with you when you come back in on Monday."

"What do you mean when I come back in on Monday? Aren't you coming back in on Monday?"

"No, I've got other things to do," replied Curly. "This will be your job. I'll help you with the beams at the other crossings, but you can handle the rest."

"How do I know where you want the other crossings?" I asked questioningly.

"We'll flag them on our way out on Friday," Curly replied.

Uh-oh, I thought to myself, this is going to be worse than digging the fence post holes. Not only do I have to work by myself until this job is over, but now I have to cook. I'll probably starve to death before this damn jeep trail is finished.

True to his word, Curly laid out the bridge crossings on Friday and on Monday he dropped me off at the trailhead. With my pack board, sleeping bag and a week's supply of groceries, I was leaving for the falls on MacKenzie Creek.

"Oh yes," said Curly as he unpacked the truck, "you're going to need this to drive the drift pins into the logs." He handed me a ten-pound sledge hammer.

Man, those drift pins and that hammer were as heavy as that bloody tent, but not quite as bulky. No problem, I wasn't going to carry them all in at once, I would make several trips.

I made no bones about it, I didn't care much for pancakes when I started work on the jeep trail, and by the time I finished it I didn't care much for Spork®, either. When a person cooks as well as I do the menu is rather lean. One can of Spork®, one can of pork and beans, mustard and bread. That sounded like the type of meal that a kid who couldn't cook should be able to rustle up with very little trouble. Besides, it made shopping real easy. I ate Spork®, pork and beans, bread and mustard or some combination of all for every meal. If that wasn't bad enough, every meal was cold.

After a few days of eating my own cooking, or as Curly would say, "can openin'", I knew what I needed real bad, even if the country didn't, and that was a forest fire. Yes sir, a forest fire and the sooner the better as far as I was concerned.

Curly was well aware of my culinary skills and what my meals consisted of when I worked alone. He hadn't mentioned anything about the empty Spork® cans that I was accumulating. It had probably just slipped Curly's mind, I reasoned, that he was going to need a fresh supply for his next victim. After every meal, I washed out each and every can and stashed it away. I figured to haul them out at the end of the project. Man, I thought, was Curly ever in for a big surprise.

"Looks like a real good job, my young friend. Well done," said Curly after he had walked the length of the jeep trail, inspecting every corner and every bridge. "We'll be able to get a jeep down here with no trouble at all now. I don't mind telling you I was a little concerned about those bridges, but they feel pretty solid. You did a fine job." We were sitting in front of the tent enjoying a cup of coffee and I wondered why Curly had walked in and not brought the jeep.

"So what do we do now that this job is finished?" I asked.

"Oh, I've got another little project planned now that this one turned out so good," Curly responded evasively.

"We going to go get the jeep now and haul our equipment out?" I asked hopefully.

"No," said Curly. "Now we're going to break camp and pack it out the same way we got it in here."

"Why would we want to do that when we've got a good jeep road in here? Please Curly, let's go and get the jeep and haul all this stuff out," I pleaded.

"Look at it this way," replied Curly. "You haul the camp in on your back, you haul it out on your back. That way you really learn to appreciate the fruits of your labour. Anyway, it won't hurt you. It'll make a man out of you. And besides, it builds character."

"Right now I could care less what it builds. I'd rather have that jeep come in here and at least pick up this damn old tent," I grumbled. Not to mention the collection of empty Spork® cans that I had jammed into my pack sack, I thought to myself.

"Well, that's life, young fella, nothin's easy. Let's go

catch us a fish for supper."

The MacKenzie Creek jeep trail was behind us, my days as a pack mule were over as we prepared for our next venture. Once again we left the ranger station in Curly's forestry green truck and I was sitting in the passenger's seat as Curly turned left and headed north on the Coal Branch Highway.

"Where we going now?" I asked Curly, not really expecting an answer. With my keen sense of observation I had already detected that Curly didn't often provide a lot of information on where he might be going or what he would be doing, particularly when it concerned me. So far, I had been told to pack my gear and take enough food for a week. I wasn't sure if that meant Curly would be cooking or I would be eating Spork®, pork and beans, mustard and bread. So I brought along five cans of Spork®, five cans of pork and beans, one jar of mustard and two loaves of bread. I was more then willing to share my grub if necessary.

A few miles north of Leyland we left the highway and turned left again onto a well-used dirt road.

"This is Craig's Lumber Road," advised Curly. "We'll be heading down to the Kaydee Cabin to check the trails out. Have to see what kind of shape they're in and clear away any windfall. After that we'll mosey on down to Craig's old sawmill site and see how things are holding up. There's still a few buildings there, never know when them old buildings might come in handy. If we have time I want to get down to the Gregg River Cabin and spend a few days there. I think we should build a jeep trail there, too. Might even get in some fishing while we're down there."

"Well, the fishing sure sounds good to me," I said, thinking to myself that a feed of fish would be a welcome change. The Spork® could stay in the can. Fresh fish with pork and beans didn't sound too bad at all. With any luck I just might get to do a little bit of rangering, but I wasn't going to hold my breath on that one.

"Did you mention jeep trail and cabin in the same breath?" I asked Curly.

"That's right. Why?" he responded.

"I was just curious, that's all," I smiled, as I envisioned myself returning to a cosy cabin in the mountains after a strenuous day of jeep trail construction. My muscles and shoulder sockets would surely give Curly a vote of thanks.

The Kaydee Cabin was a pretty new building about eight feet wide and sixteen feet long. It had two bunks, a stove, a table and a wash bench in it. There wasn't much room left for anything else. When we arrived, we took our gear inside and went for a ride to check out the trails and the surrounding country. Everything looked to be in pretty good shape. Curly indicated he was happy with it and that made me happy as well. At least there was no tent to pack in or post holes to dig.

"Looks pretty good to me," said Curly as we checked the last trail. "Let's go get our fishing poles and catch us a fish for supper."

"Hey now, that sounds real good to me," I answered.

Fishing was great in the McLeod River and it didn't take long for us to catch enough rainbow trout for supper. This had to be my lucky trip, I even got to go and catch some of the fish. I was in high spirits as I started the fire and Curly did the cooking. I didn't even mind doing the dishes. Not a bad deal for me. I could sure live with this arrangement.

I think the table and chairs and the wash table had been built by a midget. Whoever built them was quite a bit shorter then Curly and he had to bend way over whenever he used them. Curly bumped his head a lot on the lower cupboards and looked like a dog humpin' a football whenever he had to use the table or had a wash. He complained a lot about short people building things so small that a man couldn't use them without crippling himself. I didn't say a word. Things were going pretty good for me and as long as they were I was going to agree with anything that Curly said. Laying in my bunk that night, I thought to myself, I sure do like this being a ranger bit. When everything looks good, you go fishing. I could really get into this kind of work.

Next day we moved on down to Craig's old lumber camp and checked the buildings, I'm not sure what for, but we checked them. It didn't look like there had been anyone around there for a long time. The buildings were all empty except for the odd bare rough-sawn wooden tables, benches and bunk beds. Not much to check here. Then it was down to the Gregg River Cabin.

The Gregg River Cabin was a much older building and was snuggled back in the trees at the end of the pasture. It was a log cabin and the roof was built like a pyramid and covered with rubberoid roofing. The logs were weathered various shades of brown. There was a hitching rail out front for the horses that we didn't have, but it was kind of neat. It was the first time that I had ever stayed at a place that had a hitching rail. I found it fascinating and could imagine all sorts of people riding up, swinging out of the saddle, tying up their horses and coming in for a meal. I could even see their look of surprise when we fed them Spork®.

The inside of the cabin was about 16 feet by 16 feet and was much larger then the Kaydee Cabin. There were three bunk beds, a table with benches, a stove and a washstand. I could see why Curly would want to stay here. The cabin had all the comforts of home plus the added benefit of peace and quiet. No heavy hauling or roughing it here, I thought.

"Get the fire going," ordered Curly, "and while I'm starting supper you can get some water."

As soon as I got the fire going I grabbed a canvas bag and went out to find the well. There was no well out front so I walked around back and found that it wasn't there either. I searched high and low for a well and finally admitted defeat. I just knew Curly was going to think I was a real dummy having to go back in and ask him where the well was. What kind of a ranger couldn't find a well?

"There's no well," Curly laughed. "We draw our water from a little spring behind the cabin. You can follow the trail around back, past the toilet and up to the spring. You can't miss it."

"Thanks for telling me that in the first place," I said and headed off in the vicinity of the outhouse. Sure enough the trail snaked past the outhouse through the trees for about a hundred yards and came to an abrupt halt right beside a small spring. Someone had dug out a little area large enough to get the bucket in and had dropped in a number of large rocks to line the bottom.

The water was crystal clear and I could see every little detail on the bottom. I scooped a pail of water out and took a sip of it. Man, was that cold water, and did it ever taste good. Now this was living. Here was a great cabin, Curly was cooking supper and I was hauling a pail of water. What more could I ask for?

After supper we sat around the front of the cabin and had a great time feeding the whisky-jacks. They were quite tame and it wasn't long before they would come down and eat right out of our hands. Whisky-jacks provided our only source of amusement. Later on Curly said we should set up the wireless and get ready for the night sched.

"When you're out in the bush you have to check in twice a day, once in the morning and again at night. It's okay to miss one sched, but miss two and someone will come looking for you," Curly said as he got out the bulky old wireless and directed me to get a rock that I would be able to tie a string to and throw high into the branches of a tree.

"How come we never used the radio at the MacKenzie Creek falls?" I asked. It seemed strange that I spent several weeks there by myself without a radio, without any way for anybody to contact me or for that matter, for me to contact anyone.

"It wasn't important," he replied. "Anyway, you were in the shadow of the Rockies. It's too difficult to get a signal out."

"What would have happened if you'd have needed me or I had needed some help or something?"

"If I wanted you, I'd have found you," he answered, quite unconcerned.

"Yeah, I'll bet," I muttered, as I pictured Curly walking up to my half-eaten body that was being fought over by wolves and bears. Strange how I never for one second had a bit of concern while I lived in the tent at the falls. Now, that bloody radio and the sched had suddenly painted a whole different picture for me. Why would Curly be so concerned to call in when he was in the bush and yet be so apathetic when I was alone in the bush? Somehow, I didn't feel that finding me was very high on Curly's list of priorities. He was unrolling a length of wire while he talked, then started giving orders, dismissing my concerns.

"Here," he said, pointing to a length of cord, "tie this to the rock and then I want you to throw it high and through the branches of that pine tree over there. We have to be able to pull the wire up high so that we can pick up the signal when they call us."

"Gotcha," I replied and grabbed a rock. As I walked over to the tree I tied the cord to the rock and then tossed it as high as I could into the tree. The rock sailed through the branches and came down on the other side. The cord was strung over the branches just as Curly wanted. He came over and attached an insulator and the wire to the rope and pulled it into the tree, stopping just before the insulator touched the branches. Then he tied the rope to the tree trunk.

"Now take that other piece of cord and do the same thing to that tree over there," said Curly, pointing to another tree about fifty feet away. The same process was repeated and Curly attached the other end of the wire to an insulator and the rope, then added a lead wire to the main wire and hoisted them into the tree.

The lead wire was then fed into the cabin and attached to the wireless.

At the appointed time Curly attached the batteries to the wireless and turned it on. There was a tremendous amount of static and every once in a while I could hear a word or two. Then came sched time and I could hear the different district rangers report on the day's activities.

When his turn came, Curly reported that we were working out of the Gregg River Cabin, that he had been to Kaydee and Craig's Lumber Camp and everything was okay. There were no messages for Curly and he signed off. Man, was it ever exciting to be doing some real ranger-type work. I would have been in seventh heaven had it not been for the cloud of doubt cast by our latest conversation.

"I think I see how this whole thing works now," I mentioned to Curly as we sat in front of the cabin enjoying a cup of tea in the gathering dusk.

"How's that?" he asked.

"What it means to be doing real ranger-type work," I mused. "I didn't really understand it before, but just sitting here and thinking of the past few weeks has given me a pretty good idea of what it is."

"That's good," he smiled. "I'm glad, I hope that I had a hand in that."

"Oh yeah," I smiled back at him. "You can take full credit for it." That he could, I thought. When there was a lot of heavy slugging and living out in the cold and damp, Curly stayed home. When there was a nice warm cabin and no heavy work, Curly came along. Curly also made sure that he called in at sched time. He made sure that if he was missing someone would be coming to look for him. Me, I could have laid out under a tree rotting for a week and no one would have known I was gone, there was no sched for me. Yes, there appeared to be a different standard for the ranger and the grunt.

For the next day or so Curly and I worked side by side, fixing up the cabin, checking out trails and going fishing. I was basking in the glory of doing real ranger-type work. My new-found joy was short-lived. The bubble burst one morning while I was whistling my way through the dishes, wondering what exciting things Curly had on his list to do today.

"Grab that saw and pulaski tool," ordered Curly. "We've slacked off enough. Now we've got us a jeep trail to build down here."

"I should have known it was too good to last," I mumbled to myself as I followed Curly into the bush and along an old trail on the south side of the Gregg River. This time I was loaded down with the pulaski and a saw. We would be returning to the cabin for lunch. I preferred the rangering part of the job.

"We have to be able to get in here with a jeep in case of a fire," said Curly. "And don't forget, she has to be at least eight feet wide or we'll never get a jeep down it."

Now this was reality, this I could understand, suddenly I was back in the real world. At that point, I knew the gods were not on my side and I spent the rest of the summer building a jeep road on the south side of the Gregg River. The good news was the light loads, a good cabin to sleep in and Curly's cooking. Oh yes, if we missed a sched someone would come looking for us. All was right when I was part of Curly's world.

After finishing my job for the summer, I was once again sitting in the passenger's seat of the old ranger's forestry green pick-up truck headed for Edson. As we drove away from the Leyland Ranger Station, I took one last look at the garage with the large timber braces propped up behind it. I admired the empty compound that I slaved to put a fence around, assisted by the modern tool that Curly had introduced me to, the Spork® can. I felt more then just a little pride as I thought of Curly driving his jeep down one of my trails on his way to fight a raging forest fire. I was finished building fences and jeep roads for one summer and it was back to school. I told the old ranger of all the things I had done during the summer and of my experiences. He seemed to be very interested and let me do most of the talking on the drive back to Edson.

"Well, tell me, young fellow," he asked after I had expended my stories. "Do you think you'd like to do this for a living?"

"You bet," I replied, thinking that if I had the ranger's job, I'd get someone else to do the grunt work just like Curly did.

"Then you'd consider coming back again next summer?" the old ranger asked with a twinkle in his eye.

"I sure would," I blurted out. "Do you think I could?"

"Well next summer's a long way away. We'll have to wait and see. But the way things stand right now, it looks pretty good for you."

"I know one thing for sure. If I come back next year I'm gonna know how to cook. I've had enough pancakes and Spork® to last me a lifetime," I stated.

The old ranger just chuckled.

"I have a question for you. Why wouldn't Curly bring the jeep into the MacKenzie Falls and haul out the tent?" I asked. "Man, that thing was heavy. Packing it in was one thing, but to have to pack it out again was something else. Especially since the jeep trail was finished."

"Did you ever see Curly's jeep?" asked the old ranger.

"No. Can't say as I did," I replied.

"Maybe that's cause Curly doesn't have a jeep," said the old ranger.

"You're kidding me. What was he talking about then?" I asked, dumbfounded.

"Beats me," replied the old ranger and he shrugged his shoulders. "But Curly doesn't have a jeep. Never has had as far as I know."

Maybe he doesn't have a jeep, I thought, but he'll sure be surprised when he finds out he has a whole summer's supply of empty Spork® cans stashed in his garage.

THE GLENWOOD BOOTLEGGER

It was a typical Friday evening in Edson. A couple of cars drove slowly up and down Main Street, up to the water tower at the north end of town, make a U-turn, then coast down the gentle grade to the CN station at the south end of town and make another U-turn, a process that would be repeated until the vehicle was out of gas or had to be returned to daddy. Around the front of the candy store there were a half-dozen teenagers looking enviously at those with wheels on this night. Except for this beehive of activity, the streets of Edson were deserted.

There was of course the regular Friday night dance in Peers, but as usual I didn't have any wheels to get there. I quickly assessed the chances of getting a ride in one of the cruising vehicles, but they were all owned by older guys looking for younger chicks. My chances ranged from slim to none. The small crowd at the candy store, having come to the same conclusion, was busy dreaming up other possibilities. The chances of an exciting evening here did not look very promising, so I headed for the pool hall, an establishment where I spent many an evening.

There was always a game of Odd Ball in progress at the first table and if I got there early enough, before the better, big money players arrived, I stood a fair chance of picking up a few bucks. I had two dollars just burning a hole in my pocket. Two dollars that, if the right crowd was playing, I could easily turn into five or even ten. It was early enough, there was something in the air, I could just feel it. Yes, this was my lucky night.

"Yoo-hoo, Bobby Adams," came the sweetest sounding little voice, just as I started up the steps to the pool hall.

I stopped dead in my tracks. I had heard that voice often in the past. Should I turn around and look, or should I run and duck into the pool hall? "Run, you fool," my brain yelled at me. "Run, or you'll be sorry." Like a fool, I didn't listen to my brain. Instead I turned and looked around, but I couldn't see anyone else on the street. Whew, just my imagination. I chuckled and turned back towards the pool hall.

"Shame on you, Bobby Adams," cooed the voice again. "Are you trying to ignore me?"

Once more I stopped. I knew that voice, why, I even knew those words. I knew better than to stop, but like a fool I did. With all my instincts telling me to run, I turned and stupidly walked back out to the street where a number of cars were parked. Then I saw her.

"Oh no," I moaned. "I should have listened to my brain." The owner of the sweet little voice was sitting behind the steering wheel of her daddy's car with two of her friends. "Hi," I mumbled and cursed my stupidity for not running.

"Now Bobby Adams, is that any way to speak to a lady?" she asked. She batted her eyes at me and gave me her biggest smile. It was enough to make a person sick, I thought, standing awkwardly beside the car.

"What d'ya want, Margaret?" I blurted out the question. This friendliness and sweetness was not typical. Margaret's friends were somewhat older then me and neither they or Margaret ever spoke to me, unless of course I was to count the number of times Margaret had some snotty thing to say. In fact, I was surprised that outside the school house, any one of them even knew my name.

"Whatcha doin', Bobby Adams?" she asked in a voice that if I hadn't known better, could easily have been the voice of an angel.

"Gonna shoot some Odd Ball," I answered, uncertain as to whether or not I should approach the car, since Margaret was being so nice. "Why?"

"Oh, us girls were just talking about you. We're just curious, that's all," she smiled.

"Okay," I said. I was starting to feel pretty uncomfortable, even though this was not the Margaret that I had come to know. She was never this nice, although she did have a sweet little voice when she wanted to. This was too much, more than I could bear. I turned away and once more headed back towards the safety of the pool hall.

"Wouldja like to go for a ride? With us girls?" she purred in a very sweet little voice.

Would I like to go for a ride, I thought. Man, on a Friday night I'd kill to go for a ride with any one of them, even with Margaret. But now with all three, that was a dream beyond my wildest imagination.

"Yeah, I...I...I guess so," I stammered and quickly snapped around again. "Where are you...where are we going?" I asked, thinking that I could get dizzy from all the turning I was doing.

"Oh, I dunno," she cooed. "I guess, just for a ride if you'd like to come along."

"Yeah, sure. I'll come," I grinned, forgetting all about the Odd Ball game. "Yes sirree," I chuckled out loud as I walked around the front of the car. "This is my lucky day."

"Here Bob, you can sit in the front," said her friend as she bailed out of the front seat like a scalded cat.

"Oh yes," I muttered as I admired her. Just like I had always imagined when I ogled this sweet young thing from a distance, she does have the body of a goddess. I smiled as she nimbly hopped into the back seat and slammed the door before I could close it for her. "I can get in the back seat with you," I offered. "I don't mind riding in the back seat at all." I was thinking that the back seat with someone who had the body of a goddess had to be about the best seat in the car.

"No. That's okay," she fired back quickly. "You sit in the front with Margaret."

"So. Where we going?" I asked again as Margaret backed the car away from the curb and started to drive up Main Street. "Man, this is great," I sang out.

"Well Bobby Adams, where would you like to go?" Margaret asked.

"I'm goin' wherever you're going, I guess," I chuckled and turned to have a closer look at the two in the back seat. There was no doubt about it, this was my lucky day.

"Well, don't just sit there like a dummy, Bobby Adams, think of something," Margaret sneered and the twosome in the back seat giggled. Obviously Margaret had just made a funny.

"Hey, this is fine, this is great," I tooted as I stuck my elbow out the window so that everyone could see that I was in Margaret's car. Man, I could already see the looks on their faces when they looked up and saw me, Bob Adams, sitting in the front seat of the car. Yes, the car would cruise slowly up Main Street past the Edson Theatre, past the candy store where I would casually wave to the small crowd who would be staring unbelievingly. Yes, tonight I was to be one of the fortunate ones, lucky enough to have wheels to enjoy the popular pastime, cruising up and down Main Street.

I was really enjoying myself, thinking of the possibilities the evening held in store for me, when a voice in the back seat spoke. "I know," she said, "let's get something to drink."

With those words, Margaret cranked the steering wheel and stepped on the gas. Instantly the car was speeding out of town, heading west on Highway 16. We never made it as far as the Edson Theatre or the candy store. No one was going to see me in the front seat of Margaret's car.

The girls obviously had their own agenda and were in agreement that something to drink would be in order. "Hey, that sounds good, I could go for something cool right now," I agreed. "How about a coke?"

"Naw, I don't want no coke," said the voice from the back seat. "I think we should live dangerously tonight. What say we get some good stuff?"

"Sounds good to me," purred her partner. "Where we gonna get it?"

"I'll bet Bob knows where to get the really good stuff," said the gal who had vacated the front seat. The sound of her voice gave me goose bumps all over. Then she ran her fingers through my hair and everything started to get sort of fuzzy. "Don't you, Bob? You know where to get the good stuff?"

"Who, me?" I squeaked as my throat was suddenly very dry. "Sheesh, I don't know." The suggestion that I knew where to get the 'good stuff' sort of caught me a little off guard. Not being a drinker I had never really given the matter any thought, in fact, I didn't really know what the 'good stuff' was. But I had a feeling that I was about to find out.

"I know," she continued. "I hear that we can get a mickey in Glenwood for ten bucks."

"The Glenwood bootlegger," I sputtered, suddenly realizing what the 'good stuff' was. "You wanna go to the Glenwood bootlegger." I couldn't believe what I had just heard coming from the back seat. I turned and gave her a surprised look. She sat back in the seat and gave me a sly little grin. I should have listened to my brain and run, I thought. I was really beginning to sweat as I squirmed in the front seat.

"That's right, Bob. The Glenwood bootlegger," she repeated.

"Let's count our money and see if we've got enough

then," chirped Margaret as she drove west towards Glenwood. "I got two-fifty."

"We got five bucks in the back seat," added the girls in the back.

"I only got two bucks," I said in almost a whisper. Isn't that something, I thought, each of the girls has exactly two-fifty.

"That's all you got?" asked Margaret in her snotty voice as she shot me a dirty look.

"That's it, two bucks. There ain't no more," I replied with a sinking feeling.

"Dig deep, girls," giggled Margaret. "It sounds to me like Bobby Adams here can't pay his share."

I could have crawled in a hole. What had been a promising evening was suddenly taking a nasty turn. I found myself wishing that I had ignored the call and gone and played some Odd Ball. There was no doubt about it, Margaret was one despicable person.

Margaret knew exactly where she was going. She pulled the car to the side of the road a couple of hundred yards from an old shack.

"There it is," she giggled. "The Glenwood bootlegger. That's where he lives."

We all sat there and stared at the unpainted building. It didn't really look like anyone lived there. "You sure that's where he lives?" asked a voice from the back seat.

"Oh yeah, that's where he lives alright. I'm sure of that," she answered. Then she turned to me and smiled.

"Okay Bobby Adams, you're the man around here, go do your thing," she ordered.

"What do you mean, go do your thing?" I sputtered.

"I don't know what to do. I never been to a bootlegger before. I don't even drink."

"Oh, quit your snivelling. Stand up and be a man for a change," she chided. "It's easy. You just go up to the door and knock on it. When he answers, you ask for a mickey of whisky. Show him the ten dollars and give it to him when he brings the bottle. There's nothing to it," she said quite confidently.

"If it's so easy, why don't you go do it yourself?" I asked.

"I'd love to, but he won't sell to girls," she replied matter-of-factly. "Only to boys, so it looks like you're it."

"C'mon Bob," cooed the gals in the back seat. "If we're going to go to the dance at Peers tonight, we need something to drink, don't we? C'mon now, we're counting on you for a good time."

Armed with the ten dollars, I reluctantly inched my way up the steps to the door, knocked, then quickly stepped down. The girls followed, staying a couple of steps behind me. I just about crapped when the door opened and this huge pot-bellied man appeared. He stood there glaring down at me.

"Whaddaya want, kid?" growled the Glenwood bootlegger.

I couldn't speak. I just stood there looking at this huge man who was wearing only a sweatshirt. No pants, no shorts, nothing but a sweatshirt.

"Holy cow," I mumbled half out loud, "this guy's naked." I was about eye level with his waterworks, which looked like the end of a salami.

"I said, whaddaya want?" he snarled again.

"Whisky," I stammered, staring at this thing aimed at me. "Whisky. A...A...A mickey of whisky." I held out the ten dollars for him to see.

"I don't know you," he replied. "What's your name, kid?"

"Bob, Bob Adams," I answered, still not believing that someone would come to their door naked. He grabbed the money out of my hand and walked back into the house, slamming the door. I stood there like a fool. No money. No whisky. Nothing, except Margaret and her two friends.

"You weren't supposed to give him the money until you got the whisky, you dummy," Margaret shrieked. "Now what are you going to do?"

Like the dummy Margaret said I was, I pussy-footed back up the steps, reached over and knocked on the door again.

"Hold your horses," barked a voice from inside the shack. "Who the hell you think you are, anyway?" I recoiled at the sound of his voice and nearly fell off the step.

A few minutes later the door opened again and the Glenwood bootlegger reappeared. In his hand he held the sought-after mickey. He stood there staring at us, then, to everyone's relief, he handed me a mickey of whisky.

I grabbed it and turned to run, not realizing that the girls had crowded right in behind me. I plowed smack dab into the gal with the body like a goddess. I hit her with a solid check, sending us both flying. I managed to maintain my grasp on the coveted mickey as I scrambled around on the ground. I regained my feet and raced for the car and safety away from that big man, naked from the waist down, who was still standing in the doorway, laughing his head off.

"Oh my heaven, did you see what I saw?" said the gal brushing the dirt and pine needles from her clothes. "I don't believe it," she said breathlessly.

"I told you," Margaret chipped in. "Didn't I tell you? You have to see it to believe it, don't you?"

"Oh, I don't think one bottle is enough. We need another one," she said, picking the last of the pine needles from her dress. "Can we scrape up another ten bucks? C'mon girls, dig deep," she urged.

"Don't look at me," I replied. "You already got all the money I had."

Surprise, surprise. Between the three of them, the girls did indeed have another ten dollars and within minutes Bobby Adams was on his way back to the Glenwood bootlegger for another mickey. Once more I knocked on the door. Once more the big man, naked from the waist down, came to the door. But on this trip, I had company, close company. Like she had on the first visit, the gal with the body of a goddess had accompanied me, but this time she was right behind me, up the steps she came, up to the door. When the big man opened the door, she pushed right up tight against me. I could feel every inch of her body as she pressed tightly against my back, her hands on my waist, peering around my head. She was breathing hot air in my ear in an attempt to get a closer look. I could feel the temperature rising. I was starting to sweat. I don't know what the Glenwood bootlegger was doing for her, but

I knew what she was doing for me. She was driving me crazy.

"Whaddaya want now, kid?" growled the Glenwood bootlegger.

I knew I wanted the mickey, but all I could think about was this body clinging to me like glue. What I couldn't feel, I could imagine and I could feel every curve of her body pushed tight up against my back. Suddenly it was getting very uncomfortable standing in front of the bootlegger's shack. I had almost forgotten about him when he growled again.

"Whaddaya want?" he sounded impatient with me.

"Another mickey," I stammered and could feel the sweat standing out on my forehead. I handed him the additional ten dollars, which he took and again he slammed the door. I waited for him to return. The goddess clung to my back like a wet rag. Man, he was gone for an eternity, I thought as I stood there afraid to move. My mind was on — no, it was on — man, I didn't know what it was on. I didn't know what was happening to me, but the sweat streamed down my forehead.

"Why you need two bottles, kid?" the voice of the bootlegger jarred me back to reality. I hadn't noticed that he had returned to the door holding the second mickey in his hand.

"I don't know," I replied weakly. "I don't even drink. I think we're gonna have a party," I stammered, my throat getting dry. "And the girls, they don't think one bottle is enough."

"You gonna have a party with three girls and just you?" he laughed.

"Yeah, I guess so," I squeaked out weakly.

"Maybe you and the girls, you like to stay here and party with me, eh?"

"No," someone whispered in my ear.

"I don't think so," I replied as I felt the body clinging to my back shiver and press even closer. Man, but it was getting hot. I felt like my blood was about to boil.

"Listen, Bob Adams, you come back if those three girls are too much for you," laughed the Glenwood bootlegger as he handed me the mickey. Again, I would have turned and run, but I couldn't move. I was being held firmly. Finally, he closed the door and I could feel her release her grip. She turned and waltzed back to the car. Hot dog, I thought as I floated back to the car, if this is a taste of things to come, I want more. Man, but this is my lucky day.

The girls giggled and tee-heed about the naked bootlegger all the way back into town. I sat in the front seat with my arm out the window, twisting my open palm this way and that, trying to direct a little fresh air onto my sweating body as I tried to cool down. This evening had been a brand new experience for me. As I thought about the things to come, I anticipated that I'd probably even have a drink with the girls.

Suddenly my dreams were shattered when a voice from the back seat spoke up. "So where are we gonna dump the kid?" she asked.

I turned to look at her. The one who had been clinging to me like a rag only minutes earlier was suggesting they dump me. This couldn't be.

"Right here," sneered Margaret in her snotty little voice. She hit the brake peddle and the car came to a screeching halt in front of Waterloo Motors. "This looks like it's as good a place as any."

"I thought we were going to Peers to the dance?" I protested meekly.

"We are, but you're not," Margaret taunted.

"Well, I own some of the whisky," I replied.

"Yeah well, that's your tough luck, not mine. Anyway, you don't drink and even if you did, I wouldn't give you any."

"At least take me back to the pool hall," I pleaded.

"Sorry sonny. This is the end of the road for you. Out you get," she replied as cold as ice. Ah yes, in my dreams of finer things, I had forgotten this was the Margaret that I had known for years.

I figured the girls would be arriving in Peers about the same time I arrived at the pool hall. When I walked into the pool hall, the big money players were well into a lively game of Odd Ball.

"You should have been here earlier," said one of the guys I usually played pool with. He was standing back watching the game. "I had a pretty good run going until the money guys arrived. I bet I coulda taken your money, too. Man, I was hot."

"If you were so hot, you should have stayed in the game," I mumbled.

"Naw, not me. These guys are too fast for me," he countered. "Anyway, I know when I'm in over my head. C'mon sucker, I'll shoot you a game of snooker. Tonight, I'm gonna give you a lesson you won't soon forget," he warbled.

"No thanks," I replied. "I just had one."

THE MUSKEG COFFIN

Another year, another beautiful summer day. It was the first week of July and once again I was a passenger in the front seat of the old ranger's forestry green pick-up truck. Our destination was the Coal Branch. I was destined for another summer at the Leyland Ranger Station, another summer with Curly.

By the time we got to Leyland I was wishing that I had my own car. For the past four hours I had listened to the same stories I had heard the year before. Mile after winding, dust-filled mile, the old ranger relayed the same stories. I was sure that he loved to have company in that forestry green pick-up just so that he could bore them with his stories.

"Robb is a pretty small mining town," the old ranger offered. "Best mechanic on the Coal Branch runs the little garage in Robb," he would say knowingly and shake his head. "Ever want to have your car fixed, bring it to Robb. You can't go wrong." As he nattered on about the mechanic I thought to myself, sure thing, if I owned a car I wouldn't be sitting here listening to you. Right now I'd be driving myself to Leyland.

"Coalspur was a good mining town once, but now there is just the ranger station there. Not many people for the district ranger, old Charlie, to visit with any more. He sure does like to have company stop by every now and then." The old ranger said that every time we drove by the ranger station at Coalspur. He never slowed down as he checked the yard, looking for Charlie's forestry green pick-up truck. It was never there and we continued on down the highway.

"The mine in Mercoal is still running, but it will close down too now that the railroads have gone to diesel engines. Too bad," the old ranger would say, then shake his head sadly. "The Coal Branch was a great place in its day."

"Luscar is about five miles west on this road," he said, pointing up the winding road that led to the town of Luscar. "They're still mining there too, but not for long. Nobody wants coal anymore. Coal's a thing of the past. The Coal Branch is dead."

"Cadomin's dead, too, you know," the old ranger lamented with a tear in his eye. "I used to be the district ranger here. That was when this town was really alive. Mountain Park was still going then, there were lots of good rivalries between the towns with their baseball and hockey teams. The mines used to bring in the best players they could find to play. They would give them a good job, but mostly they played baseball and hockey. There wouldn't be anybody in Cadomin if Inland Cement hadn't of decided to mine limestone. That's the only thing that's keeping this town from dying now."

Somewhere along the highway my mind drifted off. I was thinking back to five years earlier when I travelled to Vernon, to Army Cadet Camp. Several of my travelling companions had been from the Coal Branch, mostly Mercoal and Cadomin. I wondered if maybe this year I would meet up with some of them. Last year had been a bust, building the jeep road.

Finally, the dust and stories were over. We had arrived at Leyland and were pulling into the compound right beside the braced garage. The first thing I noticed were those damn braces, they were still stuck to the north side of the buildings.

"Did I ever tell you about those braces on that garage there?" asked the old ranger quite seriously. "There's quite a story around those old beam braces, you know. The stories are sort of like written on the wind. Some folks have a little difficulty believing them, but I can assure you they're true. You might want to check with the young fellow that was here last year. He knows, he can tell you. Word is that he learned a lot up here last year. I'd sure check it out with him if I was you. Har har har," he roared. The old ranger just could not pass up a shot at the smart-assed kid sitting beside him. It was the happiest I'd seen him since he'd picked me up in Edson.

Not much had changed since I left last summer. The garage, the ranger station, the bunk house all looked the same. All were painted white with dark green trim, almost matching the colour of the old ranger's forestry green pick-up. Yup, everything around had been touched by the colour referred to as forestry green. Everything except the old barn which was still in need of a paint job.

The fence I had laboured over last summer was still there. Each post was three to four feet in the ground, I knew that because they were still all in a straight line. The frost had not pushed them up or to one side or the other. They had all weathered some, but they were standing right where I had planted them. The yard was exactly as I had left it, empty. Why was it still empty, I wondered?

Actually, when I really considered it, nothing had changed. One year later, everything looked the same. It was like walking back in time. There I was in the front passenger's seat of the old ranger's forestry green pick-up truck. We had just driven past the garage with its braces on the north side and had stopped beside the ranger's house. Curly was still the ranger in charge and heaven forbid, I was going to have the same roommate for another summer.

"Well, young feller." I could tell immediately he had adopted some of Curly's mannerisms. "Can you cook yet?" asked my roommate when I entered the bunk house.

"You bet your sweet ass I can," I replied, quite pleased with myself. "I learned over the winter. In fact, I can cook most anything now."

"That's good," he said, looking a little surprised. "Same deal as last year then, I'll cook 'til you complain, then you cook 'til I complain. How's that sound?"

"No deal," I replied. "All you cook is pancakes and I'll end up cooking all summer. I haven't eaten a pancake since I left here last year. In fact, I can't stand the sight of pancakes anymore. This year you cook your meals and I'll cook mine." Not everything would be the same, I smiled to myself.

First thing next morning I was ready to go to work. What works of wonder did Curly have in store for me this year? Only time would tell.

"Well, young fella, you all ready to get to work?" Curly asked.

"I guess so," I answered with guarded enthusiasm, remembering all the great things that Curly had lined up for me last year.

"I'm still trying to figure out what I'm going to do with you this year," Curly said, half-smiling to himself.

"How's the jeep trails?" I asked, not forgetting that he didn't have a jeep.

"They're fine, just fine," replied Curly.

"Are there more jeep trails to build this summer?" I asked, remembering the tent and the beam timbers.

"We'll see, we'll see," said Curly. "Right now I think we'll take a trip up to Mountain Park and see how things are up there. You ever been to Mountain Park?"

"No, we never got that far south last year. Do I have to build fences or jeep trails at Mountain Park?" I inquired cautiously.

"Not that I know of," Curly replied. "There's nothing to fence in up there and there's not much bush. You can drive a jeep anywhere up in that country," he laughed rather sarcastically. "Better pack a lunch, though," he advised me. "We could be late."

"Should I bring my sleeping bag?" I asked. I remembered that every time I got in Curly's forestry green truck last year I needed my sleeping bag along with about a hundred pounds of gear.

"We'll be back tonight," Curly said. "I just thought you might like to see what's left of Mountain Park now that everything has closed down and everyone has moved out except the hermit. I think you'll enjoy the trip. We'll leave as soon as you get your lunch packed."

We drove up the Coal Branch Highway past Cadomin. Curly pointed out the old Cadomin Collieries mine shaft and the new Inland Cement mine east of the McLeod River and the railway tracks. "They tell me they're gonna move that whole mountain," Curly said, pointing out Cadomin Mountain as we passed the new mine site.

On we drove past the Whitehorse Creek, where Curly pointed out a mountain peak in the distance.

"That mountain is right up against the Jasper Park boundary, lots of goats up there. It's a real good place to hunt." Curly had a faraway look in his eye as he stared off at that mountain.

"There's only one person lives in Mountain Park now amongst all those empty buildings. He's an old hermit and he has a jillion pack rats for company," Curly chuckled.

We slowly wound our way up the old highway, carefully skirting the washouts. "Did you know that Mountain Park has the highest railway line in the world? They tell me it used to be a real lively little mining town. Not much left now, but I thought you might like to see it anyway."

I wasn't prepared for this. Something was wrong. Curly was being real nice and even talking. Now I was really suspicious. What did Curly have up his sleeve, I wondered.

The closer we got to Mountain Park the smaller and sparser the trees got and the more my suspicions grew. There were large areas where there were only shrubs, willow and alpine meadows. It was high alpine country and different from anything I had ever seen. Curly pointed out the old mine site. The main mine buildings were still standing.

"Too dangerous to walk around there," he cautioned. We drove down the deserted streets past the remaining empty houses with their lifeless windows and doors. Some were closed, many ajar or completely gone. We looked in the old bunkhouses, homes and stores. Some of the buildings still had furniture in them, some were stripped bare. Everything was just as Curly had described it. I was in a real ghost town. It would be easy to let one's imagination run wild here.

What a weird and eerie feeling it was to walk around in the empty buildings, someone's home, someone's kitchen, their bedroom. As I walked through the buildings I could feel the hair standing on the back of my neck and I had a feeling that I was not alone. It was scary.

I was no longer interested in Mountain Park, the ghost town. Since I arrived in the lifeless town, my mind was preoccupied with the hermit. Every new building I came to I approached more cautiously than the last. In every doorway I could picture the old hermit hiding.

He had to be a scrawny old man with long, dirty, matted hair. His eyes would have a wild look, the kind you see in a cornered animal, his nose large and hooked like a beak and his teeth all rotten. He never bathed and was dirty and he had a terribly foul smell that followed him wherever he went.

The more buildings I walked up to, the greater the feeling that he would be right there. I could feel his presence, I could smell him. What would he do? The better question was, what would I do? My heart was in my mouth. The anticipation of seeing the old hermit was building with every second.

Curly knew where his house was and pointed it out to me. I could tell somebody or something lived there, but he wasn't to be seen on this day.

"He doesn't show himself unless he has to. I don't think he cares for other folks hanging around," said Curly. "He's probably sitting back somewhere just watching us."

"What are they going to do with this place now?" I asked, looking over my shoulder hoping to catch a glimpse of the hermit. I knew he was there, somewhere.

"I don't really know for sure," Curly replied. "They might burn it down or bulldoze it over. No one knows for sure. Everybody has a different idea of what should be done."

As we drove away from Mountain Park, I thought about the old hermit hiding in his house as a bulldozer pushed it over, burying him. Would he be buried alive? Would he flee if the town was set on fire? Where would he go? I would think about him for days.

Next morning Curly called over to the bunkhouse.

"Better pack a lunch — we'll be gone all day."

"Where we going today?" I asked when I got into the truck.

"The phone lines are down on the road up to the Luscar fire tower and we have to fix them."

This was my second summer there and I didn't even know there was a Luscar fire tower, let alone a telephone line to it. Boy, had I led a sheltered life the year before.

"So who uses this telephone line anyway?" I asked rather sceptically.

"I do. Other rangers do. The towermen do. It stretches all the way from the Muskeg Ranger Station in the north to the Big Grave Flats to the south. Everybody has their own ring, but if you're nosy you can listen in on everyone's calls. It's called rubbering on a party line."

"I thought you guys always used the two-way radio." I was thinking back to last summer and throwing the rock with the cord tied to it through the trees.

"We use both when they're working. It's good to have something to fall back on in case one or the other fails," he answered patiently.

Now this was not any ordinary telephone line, certainly not what I had seen strung all along the railway tracks and the highways. This line was a single strand of wire strung between growing spruce and pine trees. In some places the line was right alongside the road; in others, several hundred yards away. The line stayed in the trees.

The trees had been stripped of all of their limbs from

the ground all the way up to about four feet above where the insulator was attached. The line was actually strung on growing trees.

The line was not very far from the ground. Where it was attached to the trees, it was about twelve feet above the ground and if there was a small rise in the ground between the trees, it would be much closer. There were some places that I could barely walk under the line without touching it with my head.

"When the line is this close to the ground," said Curly, surveying a section of line that was all tangled up in shrubs and laying on the ground, "moose or elk will sometimes get their antlers caught and then they tear the line down. They can make a real mess of things. Sometimes the animal will get tangled up real bad. Some of them actually die."

We spent the rest of the week working on the line and then went on to the top of the mountain to the fire tower.

"This lookout's not very high," said Curly. "Some are built on actual towers so the towerman can see over top of the trees."

The Luscar tower was just a shack on the top of the mountain, but I could see for miles in every direction.

"If there's a forest fire out there in any direction, the towerman will be able to see it," Curly observed as he scanned the country.

Looking out from the tower as far as the eye could see there was the never-ending spruce and pine forest. The only place where trees did not exist was on the rocky slopes and alpine meadows on the tops of the mountains to the west and south. What a magnificent view and so quiet and peaceful. When Curly called out that it was time to go, I really didn't want to leave.

It was Friday evening and I lay on my bunk half-dreaming. What a great week it had been. I had been rangering with Curly all week. Not once did he give me the crappy jobs to do. We had shared each and every task. He even took the time to explain everything we were doing and why. This was my idea of rangering. Yes sir, this was the life for me, I thought as I eagerly looked forward to next week.

But like so many dreams, they were short-lived.

"Let's go, boys," I heard Curly yelling. I leapt from my bed and charged out the door. Curly was running across the yard heading for the compound. "Let's move it!" he hollered again. "We've got us a smoke."

"Where?" I yelled back and looked around the horizon. I didn't see anything.

"Luscar Tower just phoned down, he reports seeing a smoke on the Gregg River and we're going to check it out. Bring your sleeping bags. Don't worry about groceries, they'll follow us. Hustle now — we have to load the equipment and get out there on the double."

It was about 6 p.m. and Curly was all business. No fooling around here. Curly had rounded up another person to help, a Métis chap nicknamed Chief, because my roomy was nowhere to be found. Curly barked orders and we threw equipment, shovels, pulaski tools, axes, wajax bags and my favourite tent into the back of his forestry green pick-up. Now there were three in the front seat, it was a little more crowded than usual.

Curly didn't talk much as we headed down the highway and turned onto the old Craig lumber road in

146

the direction of the smoke. Every once in a while we would come over a high point in the road and in the distance we could see a thin line of dark grey smoke going straight up in the air. I remembered driving in on that same road last summer. We were heading in the direction of the Gregg River Cabin. My first thoughts were not of the fire, but the prospect of all the good food that awaited. Man, I couldn't wait for the food.

"Hope we get there in time to put her out," said Curly, bringing me back to the task at hand. "The country's awful dry right now. If it gets away from us, this one could be a dandy."

"Do you think it may be close to the Gregg River Cabin?" I asked.

"Could be," Curly replied. "Could be."

"I hope so, then we'll get to use the jeep trail. Won't we, Curly?" I asked as we sped along the dirt logging road.

"Time will tell, but I doubt it," Curly chuckled to himself.

We passed the Kaydee Cabin and continued on towards the old lumber mill until we came to a new seismic line running south-west, towards the thin column of smoke. Judging from the location of the smoke, Curly guessed that the line would take us close to the fire. We followed it to a point where it intersected another freshly cut line.

Curly paused, scanning the countryside. "Fire's right over there, I'd say about a half-a-mile away," he said, pointing to the smoke climbing out of the trees and pushing skyward.

We were on a small knoll overlooking a muskeg. "I

think we'll set up base camp here for now," Curly advised us. "I want you to set up the tent at the bottom of the hill beside that muskeg." He pointed down the line about fifty yards to the bottom of the small hill below where we were standing.

We unloaded the equipment and piled it alongside the line, then looked at Curly for further direction. Here we were almost at the fire. I was close enough to see the smoke, smell the smoke, I was rarin' to go.

"So, where do we go? What do we do? Just point us in the right direction, Curly," I warbled with enthusiasm as we stood there with our hands in our pockets and waited.

Curly looked at the tree tops before turning back to us.

"That's good. The wind's in the right direction," he said, almost to himself. "You should be safe here until I get back. For now I want you two to get the tent set up and prepare a campsite. That fire's a little too big for us to handle so I'm going back to get more men and equipment. I expect to see the camp completely set up when I get back."

"You want us to go over and start fighting the fire if you're not back once we get the camp set up?" I asked.

"I want you to stay right where you are until I get back and I don't want you going anywhere near that fire! Understand?" he snapped.

"Why not?" I asked. "I thought we were here to fight it, not sit back and watch it."

"You'll bloody well do as I say. Do you understand me?" Curly didn't sound too happy.

"Yeah. I understand," I grumbled dejectedly. I had visions of being the camp boy while others got to go fight the fire.

"Listen," Curly cautioned. "You haven't a clue about fighting fires. Now if you were to stumble up there and happen to get out in front of it, there's no telling what might happen. If that fire were to crown, you'd be dead. Right now you're behind it and there's no danger and that's the way I want to keep it. Understand?"

"Yeah, I understand. But what do you mean by crowning?" I asked. I'd never heard that term before.

"It means the fire gets into the tops or the crowns of the trees, the wind takes it and races along the tree tops. You get in front of that and you'll be fried. You won't be able to get out of the way. I don't want you getting in front of that fire and that's an order. Do you understand?"

The threat I understood, alright. It meant if I got in front of the fire and it didn't get me, then Curly would. I wasn't sure at that point which would be a worse death, the fire or Curly.

"Speaking of fried, Curly, don't forget the grub. The Chief and I will be famished by the time you get back," I mentioned. I thought it wouldn't hurt just to remind him of the priorities of those on the front line.

Curly just stared at me for a second. Then as he left to go back to town for more supplies and men he was muttering something about, "We're not going to be able to hold this baby with what we've got."

The Chief and I stood there looking at each other as Curly's forestry green half-ton disappeared down the seismic line. We spent the next hour or so dragging all the equipment Curly had dropped off down to the campsite. We were at the bottom of the hill right next to the muskeg, right where Curly wanted us. Great, I thought, if the fire doesn't get us, the mosquitoes will. There were a jillion of them, they accompanied our every move. After carting the equipment down, we set up the tent and waited.

Here we were, the first on the fire. The fire that I had prayed for all last summer had finally arrived, albeit one year late, and our task was to stand around the tent and wait. Standing around made us realize that we were getting mighty hungry from all our hard work. It sure would be nice if Curly got back with the grub, I thought.

While we were working we didn't pay much attention to the fire and just before dark we noticed that it was getting awfully smoky in the trees around us. When we checked on the wind there was nothing but pure panic in both of us. The wind had changed and was blowing the smoke right into our camp. That could mean only one thing. The fire wasn't far behind.

"You think we should try to run out of here?" I asked the Chief. He being the elder I figured right now he had to be a lot smarter.

"I don't know," he replied. His eyes were wide open and darting around like pin balls. Boy, he was as scared as I was and I was scared. I didn't know what to do, or how to do it.

"I heard once that if the fire's coming at you, you should get into some water," I said to the Chief and thereby dispensed all my knowledge of fire safety.

"Yeah, that sounds good to me," he replied, looking

around. "But there ain't no water here and I think the fire's between us and the river."

"Well, we can't stay here," I offered, "because we're in front of that fire now and if it doesn't get us, Curly will."

We both stood and looked at each other, not knowing what to do, our eyes asking the question that neither of us had the answer for. By now we could hear the fire and it was getting closer.

"I heard once that you can escape a forest fire by burying yourself in the muskeg," I said. I turned to look at the Chief for his approval, but he was already heading in the direction of the muskeg with a pulaski tool and a shovel. I followed.

We each dug a separate trench long enough for us to lay down in. The pulaski tool was used to cut along one side of the trench and across both ends. Then using the shovel we cut under the muskeg to the other side which we didn't cut, we left it as a flap. Then we dug out enough of the black oozy mud so that we could lay down and still have an airspace when we pulled the flap back over us. The trench started to fill as water slowly seeped in and turned the mud into a soupy mess. Meanwhile the air was getting thick with smoke.

"We better get in," said the Chief. "But I don't think it will matter. I think we're about to meet our ancestors."

"Now that is a comforting thought," I replied as I sat down in the sloppy ooze and started to pull the muskeg over my feet, then my legs. "Wow, is that stuff ever cold!" I said, half-out-loud to myself.

"Quit complaining," said the Chief. "It's too late for that now. Now's the time to pray."

"If we die in here they'll never find us," I said, hoping that the Chief had come up with a better idea.

"If we burn up they won't find us either," was the Chief's matter-of-fact reply.

"So you'd rather suffocate in the muskeg coffin then be baked," I remarked, thinking that if you're going to die it really didn't matter which way you went. With that I lay down in the ooze and pulled the muskeg over my head. Suffocation seemed to be a definite possibility as I squirmed around in the ooze. I had to keep my hands up in front of my face to keep from smothering.

The fire was really roaring now. Man, was I praying. Every prayer that I had ever heard came to mind and I muttered the words. All the while, I kept having this sinking feeling that I was being drawn down into the slimy ooze.

It seemed like we had been under that muskeg for an eternity, but the roaring had stopped and it seemed to be awfully quiet. "You okay?" I yelled to the Chief and from a distance I heard his muffled response.

"I think so, how about you?"

"Think it's safe to get out ?" I yelled again.

Same muffled response. "I don't know." The Chief was a man of few words.

Slowly I lifted a corner of the muskeg coffin lid. Everything was black. Of course it was black; it was night and the night air was filled with smoke. On the hill, there were a few burning branches. "I think the fire's gone," I said to the Chief. "There's not much left here."

We had been spared. The fire had passed along the ridge, missing the muskeg. We dragged ourselves out of the trenches. The ooze made a sucking sound as if reluctant to release our bodies. We were covered with ooze. As I stood up, I had this horrible uncomfortable feeling. Ooze covered my body from head to foot. I felt like I had filled my drawers. I could feel the thick ooze running down the inside of my pant leg with every step. In the night air I was beginning to feel cold and I was soaking wet.

We picked our way back to the campsite in the dark. Sure, what campsite. No need to worry about the camp, it was gone. There were only charred trees standing tall and black. Here and there a pocket of pitch continued to burn.

"I guess we might just as well sit tight for the rest of the night and keep warm. Curly will be around in the morning, he'll probably raise hell and want to know what happened to his tent," I warned the Chief.

We both knew that our prayers had been answered, by whose god, we knew not. What counted was that we were alive and there were plenty of hot spots around where we could keep warm and dry out. We had no idea how long we had been in those trenches, but it couldn't have been long because the rest of the night took an eternity to pass.

"Maybe we should go up the hill and wait at the seismic lines," said the Chief. "Maybe Curly will come looking for us tonight." That sounded good to me and we took off up the seismic trail to the intersection.

A magnificent sight met us when we got to the top of the hill. Through the smoke and haze we could see the fire. It was still crowning and it was running with the wind to the north-east towards the river. It was racing up the hill on the far side of the valley. Now I knew what Curly meant when he talked about the fire crowning. Man, did that fire go through the tops of the trees going up that hill.

The Chief and I didn't sleep much that night. We walked around to hot spots to keep warm and waited for the sun and Curly.

I couldn't believe the sight that greeted me the next morning. The Chief lay curled up beside a rock at the side of the trail. He looked like a rumpled clump of black mud laying there in the early morning sunlight.

"Man, you should see yourself," I laughed at the Chief as he stirred to life. I think most of the mud from his muskeg coffin was still clinging to him. He was the dirtiest, rattiest sight I had ever seen.

"I think you got more mud in your hair then there is in the whole muskeg," I chuckled.

When the Chief stood up, partially dried mud flaked and chipped off his clothes and fell to the ground with little thuds.

"You don't look so good yourself," he muttered. "I think you need a good bath."

My first attempt to move was accompanied by a considerable amount of pain. Dried mud clung to the hair on my legs, and every movement felt like a sharp needle. Slowly the hairs on my legs were being pulled out, one at a time. My pants still felt like they were full, this time with a huge quantity of half-dried ooze. Walking was not a comfortable exercise.

For the rest of the morning the Chief and I sat around and waited. It was the first time I had been on a forest fire and I was amazed at the damage. Mostly it had burned the small needles and smaller branches. Most of the tree trunks were still standing. They looked like silent guards of a time long past. The burned-out forest was still and quiet. Gone was the chatter of the red squirrel, gone was the call of the chickadee, gone were the whisky-jacks looking for a handout. It was real quiet and spooky amidst the smoke and ash.

The Chief and I sat around in silence. I started to think about what ifs. Man, I thought, I'm getting hungry. What if Curly doesn't get here, I could starve to death. It's already late in the day, what if he can't find which trail he left us off on? No, Curly was a good ranger, he knew his district, he knew where to find us, he'd be here soon. But what if he got trapped in the fire? Then no one would know we were there or if they did, where we were.

Curly did not come that day. He did not come that night or the next day and the Chief and I were getting damn hungry. Waiting for Curly, I had a lot of time to sit and think. My mind wandered back to the old hermit at Mountain Park. The life of a hermit had to be very lonely, I knew that for a fact. Here I was with the Chief for company and yet, I was getting pretty lonely and scared. What on earth would ever possess a man to become a hermit, I wondered. Had he, too, been on a fire and been left to fend for himself? If he did, how did he survive, what did he eat, what did he drink? Hermits probably drank swamp water, but I was no hermit and I knew that swamp water was poisonous. I had seen enough movies to know that, and I knew I would probably die if I drank swamp water.

"Swamp water's okay to drink," the Chief said between big gulps of the yellowy water he raised to his lips with mud-covered cupped hands.

"Are you sure about that?" I asked and gave the Chief a questioning glare. Maybe the Chief is the hermit, I thought. "You wouldn't happen to be from Mountain Park, would you?" I asked.

"Where's that?" asked the Chief between slurps.

"Maybe hermits don't know the names of towns," I muttered as I scooped some swamp water.

"Did you say something?" asked the Chief.

I kept my eyes on the Chief as we drank. Hermits, I suspected, were not to be trusted. We paused, then we drank some more. After leaving the muskeg, I found a nice smooth rock. With one eye on the Chief, I waited for the swamp water to take effect. I waited to die.

About noon the second day Curly had not showed up at the place where the seismic lines intersected. I didn't know about the Chief, but I had drank about all the swamp water I could hold. We couldn't wait anymore, it was obvious that Curly wasn't coming for us and we started to walk north-west along seismic lines, towards the Gregg River Cabin and the McLeod River. Walking was easier than it had been on the first day; I no longer had any hair on my legs and most of the mud had chipped off.

Somebody had to be where the fire was and the fire had to be where the smoke was, we reasoned. There was an awful lot of smoke to the north.

We didn't find anybody that day and we prepared to spend our third night in the burn. I knew that I had been lied to. Whoever said there was lots of food on a fire had never been to a fire with Curly. On this fire, there was no food, no tent, no nothing. Right now I would be only too happy to carry that tent if I could have something to eat, I thought to myself. I wish I had a can of Spork® or — perish the thought — I'd even eat a pancake. Instead, I drank more swamp water. Every time we came to a small stream, we drank fresh water. I far preferred the fresh water over the swamp.

We noticed as we walked along the seismic lines that there were patches of trees that the fire had passed by. It was refreshing to find these and rest a spell.

About midmorning on the third day we came across a familiar land mark. It was at least eight feet wide and it snaked through the forest. It was the jeep trail. Well, here was the fire that Curly had talked about. There were burned trees and small stands were no trees had been burned. The fire had been here and in some places was still burning. The jeep trail was here, but there were no fresh tracks on it. As a matter of fact, there were no tracks at all on the jeep trail. It had never been used.

"We turn right here," I said to the Chief and pointed the way down the jeep trail. "There's a forestry cabin down here about a mile." The Chief was looking at me rather strangely. He was probably wondering how I had suddenly acquired a bag of smarts. He didn't look like he was overly impressed with my sudden influx of knowledge.

"If you're so smart, how come we've been sitting up on the mountain, sleeping under the stars and drinking swamp water for the past three days?" he asked, giving me a mean look.

"It's just a guess," I replied. The Chief did not look very happy, and there was no way I was going to tell him that I spent a good part of last summer in here building this jeep trail.

The cabin and the surrounding trees had been spared. They had not burned, but evidence of the fire was everywhere, smoking stumps, smoking logs, smoking squirrel dens, there was still a lot of fire in the area and the air was heavy with smoke.

The Chief and I entered the Gregg River forestry cabin. There was no one living here, everything was bare. The bunk beds were bare, the table was bare, even the cupboards were bare. I can remember Curly saying last year, "We can't leave any food here. The mice and pack rats will eat everything we don't take out." Maybe in a moment of weakness something had been left or missed. We searched everywhere. There was nothing. That old Curly, he was as good as a vacuum cleaner when he cleaned out his cabins. The washstand was bare and there was nothing on the radio table, either. Just an old phone hanging on the wall.

Hey, maybe the phone would work. I remember Curly had said that if the lines were all up a person could talk to all the ranger stations and towers between Big Grave Flats and the Muskeg Ranger Station, which was about a hundred and fifty miles north of Leyland as the crow flies.

The telephone was an old relic of a phone, a huge wooden box about two feet long, ten inches wide and eight inches deep that hung on the wall. The receiver was a small black cone-looking affair that hung on a cradle at the side of the box and was attached to the box by a cord from inside. The transmitter stuck out of the front of the box and was permanently attached. To make a call, one would lift the receiver off of the cradle and grab the crank located on the opposite side of the box from the receiver.

There was a list of the different ranger stations and towers on the wall beside the phone. Each one had its own code. I looked up the Leyland ranger station code, took the receiver off the cradle and rang it. From some unknown corner of the west country, I heard someone lift a receiver, but no one spoke. I didn't care who answered it, I just wanted to talk to someone, anyone. I just wanted someone to come and get us.

"Hello," I yelled into the mouthpiece. "Can anyone hear me? I need help."

"Hello, hello." There was not one, but two different voices on the other end of the phone.

"Who's this?" I yelled. "Who am I talking to?" Right then I could have kissed Curly for having the foresight to fix his end of the line last week. I even took a little pride in the fact that I had helped. It may just have saved my life. I patted myself on the back.

There were two of them on the line. Curly was right, that was one thing about the forestry phone system, there were no private conversations. Anybody who picked up the line could hear and join the conversation if they had a mind to.

I had the towerman from the Athabasca Tower north of the Athabasca River on the line as well as the ranger from the Entrance Ranger Station. Hey, those guys were both north of the Athabasca River, I thought to myself. They couldn't do us any good. I told them we were on the Gregg River Fire and didn't know where the main camp was.

"Where the hell you at now?" asked the ranger.

"At the Gregg River Cabin. But there's no one here," I answered.

"That phone hasn't been working all spring," he snarled. "Are you sure you know where you're at?"

"I know where I'm at," I assured him. "I spent most of last summer in this cabin."

"Well, you get moving and get the hell out of there. That area's not safe. That bloody fire is all around you. You get moving and don't wait around for nothing, you hear me? Get out of there right now."

"That's what we've been trying to do," I countered. "You got any ideas on just how we do that?"

"Follow the road, you should find somebody along there. Now you better move it. Go on and get going."

"Man, now that's one excitable guy," I told the Chief as we started down the road towards Craig's camp. "He yelled a lot, but he didn't tell us anything we didn't already know."

From the Gregg River Cabin you had two choices of where to go. Down the road to Craig's lumber camp or back up the jeep trail and into the bush. I wondered if he thought we would be dumb enough to take the jeep trail.

We had walked about half an hour when we came across a crew putting out spot fires. They had a truck with them and we asked if we could get a ride back to the camp where Curly was, wherever that might be.

One of them was kind enough to give us a ride to Craig's Old Lumber Mill and there we found Curly and the main fire camp. There was lots of activity going on in the old camp now and all those empty buildings were being used, even the cook shack. The cook shack, man, now that was good news.

As we drove into camp, I noticed a gorilla of a man walking down the middle of the road. At the sight of the truck he stopped and took a stance, his arms held out. He was challenging the truck. The driver swung the truck out and drove around him, cussing as he did so.

Curly was standing beside the radio which had been set up outside, right beside the door to the cook shack. His back was to us when we drove in. He was pretty intent on what was being said on the radio when the truck stopped a few feet from him.

"Hey Curly," I called out. "Got anything to eat?" He turned around, the colour drained from his face. Curly looked like he had just seen a ghost. "I'm pretty hungry, Curly. Where's all this good grub you were telling me about?"

He never said a word as he charged towards me. I could see the tears in his eyes as he grabbed me in a big old bear hug, then gave me a kiss on the cheek and hugged me again. Holy Cow, I thought to myself, I was never hugged and kissed by a man before, but I sure got a mauling from Curly. I didn't expect anything like this, not from Curly anyway. This was embarrassing and I kept looking around to see who might be looking because there were a lot of people in that camp.

I was praying that there was no one I knew in camp,

which was highly unlikely because I hardly knew anybody in the Coal Branch, but I looked around just to make sure. Curly's actions were really embarrassing me, but then maybe he really liked me after all. My mother never hugged and kissed me that much and she was always really happy to see me, especially after I had been gone for a few days. So great was my embarrassment that I had almost forgotten about my hunger.

I was quite happy and relieved when Curly let me go and grabbed the Chief. Maybe he didn't like me that much after all, I thought, as I stood there watching as he gave the Chief the same mauling he had just given me. I figured maybe Curly had got something in his eyes, for he didn't seem to mind that the Chief was still coated with a healthy portion of mud. He hugged and kissed the Chief like he too was a long-lost cousin. Boy, Curly was sure emotional.

"I thought you guys were dead," Curly said several times over and over again, his eyes full of tears. "I thought you were dead. When that wind changed and the fire crowned and came back at you I thought sure you were goners," said Curly, the tears still in his eyes. "Oh, boys, boys, I'm so happy you're both okay. Are you hurt? Are you burned? Are you okay?" came his rapid-fire questions, not waiting for an answer to any of them.

"I don't know about the Chief, but I'm pretty hungry, in fact I'm starved," I said. "Right now I'll eat anything, even a cold pancake. I won't complain, either."

Curly grabbed us both around the shoulders and

bellowed "Get these boys some food," as we walked through the door to the cook house.

"It ain't meal time," growled the cook. "You eat at meal time around here."

"I said get these boys some food and I mean now," ordered Curly. I thought this old cook is going to learn that you don't fool with Curly. I was glad he was on my side, especially since I was so hungry. "There better be lots of it and it better be good and it better be hot," snarled Curly.

An older heavyset man, the bull cook, was cleaning up. He dropped what he was doing and went into the back and brought out a large plate of cold meats, pickles and bread.

"Here," he said. "This will tide you over till the cook whips something up." We were so hungry we never even said thanks. The Chief and I both grabbed food and started pushing it into our faces. Forget the hot stuff, I thought to myself, this is a feast fit for a king. The old guy went back to cleaning up.

After we ate Curly told us: "You boys just relax for a couple of days and get your bearings. There's no hurry to get out on the fire line."

"I'd like a bath and some clean clothes if that's possible out here," I asked Curly.

"Some of the younger guys take a swim in the river in the evening when they come in off the fire line. You can go now if you want. I'll have someone take you, or you can wait and go with them. I'll have some clean clothes brought out for you today."

"I think I'll get a little shut-eye and wait to go swimming until evening. Hopefully the clean clothes will be here by then," I advised Curly and the Chief and I relaxed.

At the supper table that night I had a pleasant surprise. There were several familiar faces coming in off the fire line. They were some of the guys that I had gone to cadet camp with. It was like old home week. After supper we walked west along the McLeod to a place that they had chosen for their swimming hole.

I dove into the shallow, clear icy waters of the McLeod River. The initial shock just about took my breath away. I gasped for breath as I struggled to gain my footing on the rocky bottom.

"Man, are you ever dirty," laughed one of the boys. "Look what you're doing to the river."

A small eddy had formed on the downstream side of my body and bits of clay and crude were swirling around. The water flowing away was a sharp contrast to the rest of the crystal clear river.

Curly had been right about that fire. It got away and it was a bad one. We heard at the fire camp that it was threatening to burn the town of Mercoal and there was talk of evacuating it. That caused quite a stir in camp. Most of the fire-fighters came from Mercoal. They had an added incentive for stopping the fire.

Some talked of how they got conscripted. "I was at the theatre with my family," one guy was saying. "Suddenly, halfway through the show the lights came on and two rangers walked in the front door. I knew what that meant and left my family sitting there and took off out the rear exit. Them sneaky bastards had the police back there with a couple of trucks. I was loaded onto the back of the trucks with everybody else and brought out here." Others had been picked up just walking down the street and a couple complained that they were coming out of church when they were nailed. Everybody was griping and complaining about having to fight the fire, but they were all having a good time.

It was good to be in the company of old friends. In fact, it was good to be alive.

The camp was a beehive of activity the next morning as the crews were getting ready to get back on the lines. I lay in bed relaxing. There was no hurry for me, after the rush would be soon enough to enjoy a leisurely breakfast.

I left the bunk house and started for the cook shack. The Gorilla was walking down the road towards me and he motioned me over, but the cook shack was closer and had more appeal. I turned and went in. The heavyset bull cook came over and inquired about my health and gave me a coffee. Then he served up bacon and eggs, ham, fried spuds, toast and a can of peaches. I ate like a pig and enjoyed every minute of it. Now this is fire-fighting, I thought to myself, no wonder I prayed for this all last year.

After breakfast, I decided to take a little tour of the camp. It would be nice to see what was there. Most of the guys were out on the fire by now and there were only a few people left. They were needed around the camp to keep things running. Since I was something of a wheel, or at least I figured I was, I thought I'd just check in on everybody and see what they were doing.

Back on the road, I headed for a bunch of vehicles where there were a half-dozen guys working. I'd start there and bless them with my presence. The Gorilla was

165

still patrolling the road and once more he motioned me to come over.

What the heck, I thought, the mechanics could wait. I walked over and stuck out my hand. I might as well meet the Gorilla first.

"Bob Adams," I introduced myself and stepped towards him. The Gorilla immediately crouched, his arms extended, ready to do battle.

"I'd stay clear of the wrestler if I was you. He ain't quite right in the head," called the friendly bull cook. "Mess with him and you're just asking for a heap of trouble."

"Thanks for the warning," I replied as I retreated back towards the cook shack and safety. It seemed to me the bull cook was always around when I needed help. Maybe he was my guardian angel, I thought. I turned to thank him again, but he was nowhere in sight.

After a couple of days of laying around, dodging the Gorilla, waiting to join the boys for the nightly swim, gorging myself at every meal and in between as well, I was getting bored. I was ready to get back out and do some work and I reported to Curly.

"Good, I've got just the job for you," Curly responded and smiled. "Come on with me. I think you'll like it." We left the cook shack. Right outside the front door we stopped and Curly said, "You're our new radio operator. You have to be here all the time and take or send all messages. You'll also have to take the sched. Think you can handle it?"

"Yeah, I can handle it," I grumbled. "But why me? How come I can't go out on the fire line with everyone else? I'd really like to go out with the guys I know."

"You've provided me with enough excitement for one lifetime. One close call is all I can take," Curly said, almost whispering. He walked away.

Working the radio did have its advantages. It kept me away from the road and the Gorilla and I got to meet everybody in the camp. They all had to pass me to get into the cook shack.

The best mechanic on the Coal Branch was in charge of keeping the vehicles running. Every day he would bring me a list of parts and materials that were needed. I would take the list and send the orders.

Another day a slim elderly forest officer who I had never seen before came up and asked if I could send a message and then gave me some very specific instructions.

"No problem," I responded and took the message as he walked away. I read the message and then noticed the name at the bottom of the page: Charlie. "Hey Charlie," I called after him, but he was gone. I was gonna introduce myself and tell him that I had driven by his place several times with the old ranger, but that he was never around. Now he was gone again.

Special privileges were also accorded the person manning the radio out in front of the cook shack. The bull cook would often stop on his frequent trips in and out of the cook shack. He would drop off a slice of pie, a piece of cake, coffee or juice. He never said anything, he would just set it down and leave. He wasn't like the others working around the camp in that he was always clean-shaven. It seemed that everyone else had used the fire as an opportunity to grow a beard.

Finally, the fire was declared under control and the

mop-up completed by mid-August. As the camp was breaking up, Curly had me help out with some of the time sheets. I had to go make sure that the names and addresses were correct so that the checks could be sent to the right place. I had almost completed my latest task, but had to report back to Curly that the bull cook had already left camp and I didn't have his full name or address.

"That's okay," Curly replied. "I know his name. I'll fill it in later."

"Yeah, but what about his address? Where you gonna send his check to?" I was concerned for the friendly guy who had insured that I always had lots to eat.

"I'll just have them mail it to me and I'll drop it off for him the next time I go to Mountain Park," Curly smiled.

I just stood there and stared at Curly, thinking about the heavyset, clean-shaven man who had brought me coffee and cake all summer. He was such a quiet man. He was the hermit!

HAIR CREAM,
THE GREASY KID STUFF

I stood there, speechless, staring at the man. He, on the other hand, sat on what I presumed was a stool, behind the wicket, grinning like a skunk on a gut wagon. This man was obviously enjoying himself immensely while I squirmed. Sweat and hair cream, the greasy kid stuff, joined forces and streamed down both sides of my face. What had started out to be a fantastic evening, the kind of evening that dreams are made of, had suddenly taken a turn — a very bad turn — and I was bearing the brunt of it. This man, with a grin from ear to ear, was turning my dream into a nightmare. A nightmare of monumental proportions.

The past year suddenly flashed through my head as I recalled why I now found myself in this embarrassing predicament. I remembered how proud and happy I had been when I landed the job with Forestry. Not because of any particular skills I possessed that related to the job, no, I got the job because I could play baseball. Yes sir, I, Bob Adams, had been given the job of Assistant Clerk in the Edson Forest headquarters. I finished Grade 12, played right field for the Edson Athletics in the July 1st, Dominion Day, baseball tournament, then I started work. Right in Edson, too. I didn't even have to move away. I was able to stay right at home, in my own bed. My meals were cooked for me every day. No more pancakes. My laundry was done regularly, clean clothes every day. Best of all, I didn't have to pay rent. Yes, life was indeed a bowl of cherries. Man, but I had it made.

Edson High School also had a pretty good basketball team that year. I sure wanted to be a part of the team for another year. Lucky me, Hank, the Forest Superintendent, was kind enough to give me time off to upgrade one subject. That one subject made me eligible to play basketball for one more year. When school started in September, I, Bob Adams, student, attended the first class in the morning. With my studies over for the day, I would walk to the Forestry Office and work until noon. At noon, I would often duck into the pool hall for a couple of quick games of snooker, then race back to work until 5:00 p.m. After supper, I would either return to the pool hall or to school to practice basketball.

Being a working man, I had, of course, come up in the world. I often had enough money to do what I wanted, as long as it didn't cost very much. I could, if so moved, go to the theatre to see a movie, any night of the week. It was as simple as walking in and plunking down my quarter. And that to me was the best part of it, plunking down a quarter, student fare, because I was still going to school. Ah yes, because of one class a day, I got to play basketball and get into the movies for a cheaper rate. The man behind the wicket often scowled at me and I could sense how badly he wanted to charge me for an adult ticket, but after all I was a student. He really didn't like it, but the student fare prevailed. Oh indeed, when one had a permanent job, it was a great life, but having a permanent job and being a student was an even greater life.

I was not alone in upgrading my education. There was another young fellow in Edson who was also taking one morning class. We would talk about nothing, about everything, solving the problems of the world as we strolled downtown kicking small rocks, pebbles or cans off the sidewalk. Now, this fellow, my classmate, happened to have an older sister and she was an absolute beauty. The fact that she was a few years older was not lost on me. I had often seen her from a distance and had cast a longing, wanting eye in her direction. An eye, I might add, that had absolutely no hope of getting anything more then severely blackened for being so bold and foolish. But then, I was a working man now and who could tell what the future held in store for me? Might it be this beauty? Maybe someday, someday....

One fine spring day love was in the air. It was everywhere, the world was full of the sights and sounds of love. Birds in the trees were singing their little heads off as they flitted through the branches. Bees, busy collecting pollen to make honey, were buzzing wildly as they darted around the deliciously scented lilacs. Young

Bob Adams was feeling his oats. So strong was the feeling, the urge, the drive, so light-headed and out-of-touch with reality was I that while walking past the lilac trees with my classmate, I foolishly blurted out: "I think I'll phone your sister tonight and take her to a movie."

My classmate, too, may have been smitten with the birds and the bees, not to mention the scent of the lilacs, for he either hadn't heard my bold statement or chose to ignore it. He just continued to walk along, then stepped off the sidewalk to kick at a rusty old can. He too acted as if he owned the world.

As the scent of the lilacs drifted away and my head started to clear, I decided that maybe I had best forget the whole thing. The farther I got from the lilacs and the closer to the office, the more thankful I was that his hearing was not all that good. Once at the office I forgot all about the birds and the bees and the local beauty. I settled into the daily routine and topped my day off with a visit to the pool hall.

I was soon to find out that my classmate's hearing was actually quite a bit better than I had originally thought. On our walk from school the very next day, as we were once more passing the lilacs where the birds were singing, the bees were buzzing and the perfumed scent drifted on the breeze, my classmate spoke. It was a sort of delayed reaction to my revelation a day earlier.

"You know, Adams, my sister is more than just a little annoyed with you right now," he suddenly interjected into the soothing sounds of mother nature.

Now it was my turn to walk along like I hadn't heard a word he said. But I had. So, he's not deaf, I mumbled to myself as we passed the lilacs. Instantly I could feel my temperature rising as the peaceful summer day began to get clammy and took on a whole new perspective. Why, I didn't even think that she knew I existed, let alone knew enough about me to be annoyed. As my heart bounced around like a pin-ball, I looked at him out of the corner of my eye. Was he for real, or just pulling my leg? He was just strolling along as if nothing, not a single word, had been spoken. My brain was racing wildly as I tried desperately to think of what I had done to make her notice me. It must have been pretty good, whatever it was, good enough to annoy her.

"Why, what did I do?" was the most intelligent thing I finally managed to squeak out.

"You stood her up, that's what," he replied quite calmly before kicking at a small stone and sending it flying back onto the street where it had probably come from. "My sister doesn't like to be stood up."

"What do you mean, I stood her up? I've never even spoken to your sister. How could I stand her up?"

"You said you were gonna phone her up and take her to a movie. Didn't ya?"

"Ya, well I didn't," I countered.

"Ya well, I told her you was gonna call her last night and take her to a movie. She got all dressed up and everything. Then you didn't call or show up."

Upon arriving at the door leading into the candy store, without so much as a goodbye, my classmate turned and went inside. I continued on, to Forestry headquarters. His words, 'my sister is more then just a little annoyed with you', kept ringing in my ears.

Later that afternoon, I was experiencing just a mite

of trouble keeping my mind on the onerous tasks assigned to the assistant clerk in Edson Forest office. I was having a terrible argument with myself. Should I phone and make a complete fool of myself or should I mind my own business and run the risk of being publicly chastised by one of Edson's beauties the next time our paths crossed?

Stupidity seemed to be the order of the day and finally won out over common sense. What the heck, I argued with myself. The worst that can happen is she will die laughing when she says no. After the rejection, in order to avoid the embarrassment that was sure to follow when I next met her, I would then spend all of my time in the pool hall. That was a safe place, like a sanctuary, it was the one place that girls never entered. On the other hand, she might say yes.

I picked up the phone and gave it a good crank.

"Number please," asked the operator in a tone that suggested it had been a long, long day. As soon as I gave her the four-digit number, I knew I had made a drastic mistake.

"Oh, hi Bob. How are you today?" she asked, her voice suddenly becoming very sweet and friendly. "Just a minute and I'll connect you. Talk to you later. Bye now," she cooed as the phone began to ring.

Stupid. Stupid. Stupid. I mumbled as I waited for someone to answer the phone. I knew the operator was listening in and that every operator on duty would also be privy to my conversation. After all, listening in on other people's conversations was all part of the job for telephone operators. I think that must have been the most important part of their training. All the ones I knew, and I knew every one of them, were very, very good at it.

To my amazement, not only was my classmate's sister expecting my call, but she informed me that she would be happy to go to a movie with me and yes, that very night would be ideal.

Now that the unlikely event was about to happen, I frantically dug deep into my pockets and rummaged through my wallet. As usual, finances, or lack thereof, were one of my major stumbling blocks. I spread the few coins I had out on the desk and very carefully counted them.

"Let's see now," I mumbled out loud. "If she doesn't eat too much, I have just enough money to pay for two tickets, two adult tickets, a box of popcorn and a soda. But we're going to have to share the popcorn and soda." I was sure hoping that she would share, because I had become rather fond of popcorn and soda pop while watching movies, and I couldn't afford two of each. No matter how I counted that money, I could only afford two tickets, two adult tickets, I had to keep reminding myself, one popcorn and one soda. That was the extent of my bankroll and after my big date, I would once again be flat broke.

Returning the coins to my pocket, I had a vision. It was the man at the ticket wicket at the theatre. He was sitting there, gloating as he sold me two adult tickets. He had been trying for the whole year to get me to buy an adult ticket, but I had always managed to get by on the student's fare. Now he had his chance. I was going to have to buy an adult ticket. Worse yet, I had done it to myself. Then it hit me. It was even worse then I first thought. Once I bought an adult ticket, I would have to buy an adult ticket all the time. Man, this stupid date was going to end up costing me a bundle.

After work, there was no thought of dropping in at the pool hall for a quick game of snooker. I had places to go and things to do, there was certainly no time to waste. I ran all the way home. I gulped down my supper. Much to everyone else's surprise, I took a bath, and it wasn't even Saturday. I brushed my teeth and worked feverishly to get my brush cut to stand up, straight up. I put enough hair cream on those stubborn blonde locks to grease a locomotive, but the cow-licks refused to give in. They swirled every which way on the top of my head in an undying effort to avoid standing on end.

I searched through my closet for my best clothes. After all, I reasoned, if I was going to take one of the best-looking girls in Edson to the movies, I had to dress the part.

By a quarter to six, I was ready to go. I still had an hour or so to wait, but I was ready. I sat in my bedroom with my jacket on and waited. I sweated and I waited. It felt like the sweat and the greasy hair cream were both running down my face in great rivers. But still I sat. I waited and I sweated until it was finally time to go.

It seemed to me like I floated all the way to her house, although to others it may have appeared like I stumbled or tripped on every pebble and line on the sidewalk, for I had to make several hasty recoveries to maintain my balance as I made my way across town.

"I see you didn't stand me up this time," she chuckled when she opened the door.

I couldn't believe my eyes. I knew instantly that this bold step I had taken, a quantum leap for little Bobby Adams from the stump farm, had been a bad idea, a very bad idea. I stood there staring, feeling hopelessly out-classed. Suddenly I wished I were back in the safety of the pool hall.

Standing before me in the doorway was the most beautiful girl I had ever seen. She was more beautiful than I had ever imagined and she was dressed to the nines. High-heeled shoes, nylons, a beautiful dress cut from cloth that looked like it had just come out of a flower garden, a soft fluffy pink sweater draped over her shoulders and her hair combed to perfection, not a single strand out of place. My date for the movies looked like a doll. No…she looked like a movie star.

I, on the other hand, stood just outside the door. My shoes were an old pair of runners that I had kicking around and had obviously kicked around. They looked like something that might have been retrieved from the town dump. I was wearing my best jeans, they only had one patch on the knee.

"There's lots of good wearing in those pants yet," Mom had said when I asked about getting another pair. I did have on a brand new white T-shirt, though, as well as my Edson Athletics baseball jacket which was only a couple of years old. Standing outside the door before the gorgeous lady that was my date for the evening, all I could do was stare. Stare while the sweat and hair cream streamed off the top of my head and down the side of my face. I was thunderstruck. I couldn't think of a word to say. I couldn't believe my incredible luck.

"Shall we go?" she asked, stepping outside and taking my arm. It took me a couple of seconds for the words and the touch to register. Good thing she took my arm, I thought, in my state I'd never have thought to give it to her.

I didn't have wheels. They were something I could only dream of, but then one never knew, one dream was certainly coming true. This dream was walking right beside me. Arm-in-arm we walked, for all the town to see, along the streets of Edson all the way to the theatre. She walked and talked. I, too, was walking. I was grinning. I was sweating like a hog. But, you know, I was willing to be that hog, because I knew that no one could wipe the smile off my face, not even with a dirty rag.

Inside the theatre, the man at the ticket wicket looked up. He did a double take, shocked at the sight of the unlikely couple moving towards him. He gave us a knowing smile, then he turned to me and I could see the evil in his eye. He knew he had me. Finally he was going to get his pound of flesh and he couldn't wait. But I was ready for him, I had already resigned myself to the fact that I would never get into the theatre for student fare again. From now on, I, Bob Adams, was an adult and I would have to pay the price. Tonight, I had crossed the barrier. There was to be no return.

"Two adult tickets." I spoke loud enough to make sure he knew that I knew the jig was up. That ought to take the wind out of his sails, I chuckled to myself.

"One adult and one student," he bellowed, loud enough for the whole town to hear.

"Huh?" I blurted out, not believing what I had just heard. I cast a quick glance at my date as her hand slipped from my arm.

"No! No! Two adults," I repeated quickly and not nearly as loud or as confidently as I had been seconds earlier. "I'm a working man now. I have a full-time job. I'm an adult."

"I know," he said and smiled back, giving me his best 'I gotcha' smile. "One adult and one student, or if you'd like, since you're with an adult tonight, I could give you a child's ticket, but that would be just for this one night. I'm sure you understand."

I nodded pathetically as I wiped the sweat and hair cream, the greasy kid stuff from my face.

I HAD A CAST-IRON GUT!

My friends were green with envy and they were in a joyous mood as they swarmed the door of the little airplane.

"C'mon, Adams," one of them called out. "Get your lazy butt out of there and tell us what it was like."

"Yeah, c'mon. Hurry up," someone else yelled. "We haven't got all day."

"What's the matter with you anyway?" called a third as he peered through the window for a better look at me.

I, having just returned from a flight over the forest fire that was raging north of Edson, was still sitting in the little airplane long after everyone else had left. My friends had been there to see me off. An hour earlier they had oohed and ahhed as I boldly strode towards the airplane with the pilot and a Forest Ranger for a reconnaissance flight over the fire. I was somewhat of a hero to my friends, for I was the first of the group to even sit in an airplane, let alone fly in one.

Sitting alone, I wondered how on earth I had come to be in this predicament. Slowly it came back to me.

The fire had been burning for more than a week

north of Edson, up towards the Athabasca River. I, being the assistant clerk in the Edson Forest, had the enviable job of processing the mounting stack of invoices that were rolling in. Man, how I yearned to get out on the line. To be where the men were, where the excitement was, to be a part of the action. I had to admit, though, that I did get to call the grocery store for the latest order of grub, but like everything else this too was done from the relative safety of my desk. I had watched daily as others had come and gone, gone to the front line, gone to fight the fire. I longed to get in on the action, but such was not the case for someone with the lofty position of assistant clerk.

Yesterday, I had been fortunate enough to overhear a conversation in the lunch room. One of the rangers was going to be flying over the fire, early in the morning. He was going to assess the damage and estimate the size of the burn. That was my chance, and I only needed one, for I had something that I concluded would be very useful. I had an 8-mm movie camera, and if I did say so myself, I took a pretty good picture.

"I can take my movie camera along and film the fire for you." I interrupted the conversation with my proposal.

They all stopped talking and looked at me. Then the Superintendent asked the ranger, "Do you think you got room for one more in the plane?"

"Well," he started, then paused. "We could certainly use the camera, but I'm not sure we need the kid."

"I thought there was just you and the pilot going up," stated the Superintendent. "Who are you planning on filling the back seat with?"

"Well, uh…nobody, I guess," he stammered. "I just don't think the fire is any place for the kid, that's all."

"I been on fires before," I countered. "I spent the last two summers fighting fires and on the front line, too."

"I think maybe you could probably squeeze one more into the back seat if you try," replied the Superintendent. "After all, it is built for two."

"I'll go get my camera and some extra film," I yelled as I raced from the room.

"You better be there at 8 sharp tomorrow morning, or we're leaving without you," an unhappy ranger yelled after me.

That night I told all my friends, "I'll be flying tomorrow. The Superintendent wants me to film the fire. I'll be going up at 8 a.m. sharp." Yup, I was a pretty important guy. I had a lot of responsibility and I was letting everyone who cared to listen know.

At 6 a.m. I was at the airport, standing beside the plane. I was the only one there—not even the pilot had showed up—but the water bombers were there. They were a new concept in fighting fires and were drawing a lot of attention. The pilots of the water bombers were really looked up to, they were the real heroes. They would come back from each run and as their planes were being loaded for a second run, they would entertain us with tales of swooping in over the fire, barely missing the treetops, flying through the smoke and flame to drop their loads. Oh, it was an exciting time. As I stood in awe, I realized that sitting in the office every day, I was missing all of the fun things in life. But not today; today I was to be a part of the action. I waited for the pilot and the ranger.

By 8 o'clock, a number of my friends had showed up. Some were there, I'm sure, to see if I was on the level; others just wanted to say they knew someone who had been in an airplane.

Man, was I important that morning as I strutted around. I had even worn my little felt Swiss type mountaineer hat. It sat, perched on my head like a beacon for all to see. I stood out from the rest, of that there was no doubt. I was on top of the world. Clutching my little 8-mm movie camera, I crawled into the back seat and the pilot explained the rules to me. I was eager to learn. I did up my seat belt exactly as instructed. I even took a casual look at the barf bag. No need for that, I assured myself, I had a cast-iron gut, a constitution like a horse.

"Remember," the pilot had cautioned me, "everyone on this plane is responsible for their own mess. If you have to puke, you use the barf bag, you understand what I'm saying?"

"Gotcha," I laughed. I wondered who the pilot thought he had, some sissy kid?

"You puke in the back of my plane, you clean it up," he cautioned again.

As the little plane taxied to the end of the runway for takeoff I could see my friends waving and shouting at me. They were a pretty excited crew. I waved back and lifted my camera to remind them that this was not just a free ride, I would be earning my way. I had been designated to film the fire.

What a tremendous sensation I experienced when the wheels left the runway and the plane lifted off the ground. Up over the tops of the trees, suddenly I could see the whole town of Edson. I could even see our house. I could not control the urge to wave, so I waved at a house with nobody outside. Nobody could see me, but I waved anyway. The houses and farms, the fields and the muskegs, places where I had often walked, where I had trapped squirrels and shot chickens, they all unfolded before me. It was a new world, a world that I knew very well from the ground, but a world I was seeing for the first time from the air.

In the distance I could see the smoke billowing up from the fire. I grabbed my camera and started to roll the film, after all that was why I was there. Filming the fire was my sole reason for being on board this beautiful morning.

As we neared the fire, the pilot advised us that there was a water bomber approaching for a run. "What say we follow him in and see how that stuff works," he stated. "Is everyone game?"

"Take 'er in, captain," I yelled back enthusiastically. "The film's rolling."

The plane banked and the little plane seemed to stand on one wing as it spun around. I was looking through the viewfinder, desperately trying to find the water bomber. All I could see was the trees, smoke, clouds and sky whizzing past in a blur that resembled absolutely nothing I had ever seen or experienced before.

"I can't find the water bomber," I shouted out as the scene in the viewfinder suddenly showed nothing but smoke and the odd orange-yellow streak as a flame licked through.

"It's right in front of us," yelled the pilot. "We're

following him in right now." It seemed to me that the little plane suddenly stood on its nose, then dove right towards the ground.

"Whattaya think you're doing?" I yelled and dropped the camera. I stared out of the front of the window at the trees coming up to meet us at a dizzying pace.

"Get this on film," the ranger barked at me. He too seemed to have his eyes glued to the spot where we were going to crash.

"Film it yourself," I yelled and closed my eyes. Then I felt like I was being pushed down into my seat as the pilot pulled the plane out of the dive. Instantly we were going up, back into the sky. I picked up my camera and looked out the side window at the trees and the smoke that we were leaving behind.

"Did you get that?" asked the ranger as he turned to look at me with a big grin on his face.

"Oh yeah, I got it alright...I think I got it," I mumbled. He was smiling now, but he sure wasn't smiling when we were heading for the ground.

"There's a hot spot over there," called the pilot. "Man, look at that thing flare up. Get a shot of that if you can."

"Got it," I replied as I snapped the camera up to my eye. At that precise moment the pilot chose to stand the plane on one wing again. Once more the countryside went whizzing around the inside of the camera as I searched for the hot spot. Man, I thought, with this plane dipping and diving all over the place, I was never going to get any good pictures. All of a sudden a clump of large trees loomed up in the viewfinder, then just as quickly disappeared in a blur of colour and I realized we were once more flying over the fire, just skimming the treetops. Everything was dipping and diving and whizzing around so fast I was having a devil of a time finding anything.

It was about that time that I received another message. It was not a message from the pilot or the ranger, it was a message from my cast-iron gut. In the blur of everything that was happening, I realized that my gut was also spinning and whirling around. In fact it was spinning so darned fast that I knew instantly I was going to puke. The words "you clean up your own mess" came bouncing through my brain as I looked for the barf bag. What a horrible discovery I was about to make. When I took my eye away from the viewfinder, I became aware of the fact that everything on the inside of that little plane was spinning around like a top. I couldn't find the barf bag, and I didn't have time to search for it.

My mouth was suddenly full of puke. The only thing that seemed to be where it was supposed to be was the little Swiss mountaineer hat. It was still perched on top of my head, a noble symbol of my great importance. I dropped the camera and grabbed for the hat as puke began to drip out of the corners of my mouth and heaven forbid, it was also coming out of my nostrils. Then, in the back seat of the little airplane, all by my lonesome, I proceeded to puke my guts out, right into the fancy black hat.

The pilot and the ranger continued to evaluate the magnitude of the fire. The little plane dipped and dived, this way and that, chasing one hot spot after the other.

The fire no longer held any interest for me. As far as I was concerned the whole country could burn. I wanted out. I had not looked out the side window since I began to fill up my hat. My only thought was to keep from dying. On second thought, maybe dying wouldn't be such a bad idea after all.

I slumped forward in the seat, and held the hat gingerly with both hands. My face was almost buried in the contents, but I was too sick to try to lift my head. As the plane stood first on one wing tip then the other, I tried my best to keep the contents I was depositing with great regularity in the hat. With each gut-tearing retch, the bacon, eggs, coffee and toast I had for breakfast splashed into the mess which rose ever closer to the rim.

If the sight of my half-digested breakfast wasn't enough to gag a maggot, the smell certainly would have finished him off. The more the plane turned and dived, the more I prayed for a swift sudden end. Please Lord, I prayed, let me die.

"Okay kid, you can get out now," the ranger laughed. I retched again as I thought of the sick joke he had just made.

"You be careful with that hat," added the pilot. "I don't want none of your breakfast decorating the inside of my plane. Remember, spill one drop and you clean it up."

"When do we land?" I sputtered through the strings of puke that hung from my mouth and nose. I was afraid to lift my head to look around in the spinning, twisting, turning plane. I feared that any movement would cause great gobs to plunge to the floor.

"We've landed, kid," laughed the ranger again. "I'm

glad he came along," I heard him say to the pilot. "I haven't enjoyed a flight like that in a long time. I love to see these rookies get a good lesson."

The inside of the plane was still moving, spinning like a top, as I tried to lift my head and move my feet. My head hurt like crazy, my stomach muscles screamed from all the retching and my feet felt like lead.

"Can someone help me?" I asked meekly, pleading for help. "My legs don't seem to be working too good."

"Well, your gut seems to be working overtime. You better learn to help yourself. Around here, every man helps himself," the ranger roared.

"But I don't want to spill any of this," I pleaded.

"Don't worry about it," he chuckled. "If you spill it, you can clean it up."

Somewhere in the distance, I could hear voices, familiar voices. They were laughing excitedly as they got nearer. It was my friends. They had come to welcome me back to earth to hear all the wonderful things I had seen and done.

"I wouldn't touch that door if I was you," I heard the ranger say. "You may get covered in puke if the great photographer ever figures out how to turn the handle."

I sat in the seat, my nose just inches above the slop in the hat. The smell was still causing me to retch uncontrollably. I was craving a breath of fresh air, air that was only inches away, but seemingly beyond reach. Finally, I mustered up enough courage to try to flip the handle with my elbow.

Very carefully I lifted my elbow up towards the door latch and leaned over slowly, carefully. Try as I might,

I couldn't unlatch the door and I rested my elbow on the window sill. Suddenly a gush of fresh air hit me. It was like a gift from the gods, cool and refreshing.

Outside, the familiar voices hushed, then there was a roar of laugher. The sound of the voices and the fresh air helped to renew my spirits. I was feeling better. I lifted my head and looked out the window. To my horror, I realized that something was protruding from the window of the plane. That something was what had allowed the fresh air to pour into the plane, it was…my elbow. I had shoved my elbow right through the flimsy side window of the plane. Once again I was sick as a dog. I dropped my head into the cap for another putrid smell and retched again.

Finally, I was able to get the door open without spilling any of the contents of my Swiss mountaineering hat in the plane. I feebly chucked the hat and contents out onto the ground as my friends whooped and howled. I crawled out of the plane and staggered a couple of steps before falling. Out in the fresh air, away from the smell, I finally quit retching.

I lay on the ground, thankful that the eventful flight had finally ended. Oh man, I moaned, as I lay there near death. Nothing like this had happened to me on the stump farm, well not since Larry and I had tried the ceegars and the beer, anyway. If this was what working in the real world was like, I'd had enough to last me a lifetime.

ROBERT J. (BOB) ADAMS

Bob Adams was born in Turner Valley, Alberta in 1938. He grew up in the Edson area, in a log house, built by his father on a farm rich in swamp spruce, tamarack, willows and muskeg.

Bob, an avid outdoorsman, was one of the fortunate few who was able to live his boyhood dreams as he entered the workforce. In 1960, after a number of years with the Alberta Forest Service and Royal Canadian Mounted Police, he began a career with the Provincial Government as a Fish and Wildlife Officer. For the next 33 years, he found his homes to include Brooks, Strathmore, Hinton, Calgary, Peace River and Edmonton.

In 1993, after a full career in Enforcement, he retired from Fish and Wildlife and wrote his first book, The Stump Farm. Today, Bob resides in Edmonton, Alberta with his wife Martha where he continues to work on his writing.

GIVE A "ROBERT J. ADAMS" BOOK TO A FRIEND

Megamy Publishing Ltd.
Box 3507
Spruce Grove, AB   T7X 3A7

Send to:

Name:_____

Street:_____

City:_____

Province/   Postal/
State:_____ Zip Code:_____

Please send:

"The Stump Farm"   @ $16.95 =_____

"Beyond the Stump Farm"   @ $16.95 =_____

"Horse Cop"   @ $16.95 =_____

"Fish Cop"   @ $16.95 =_____

"The Elephant's Trunk"   @ $15.95 =_____

"The South Road"   @ $16.95 =_____

"Skunks and Hound Dogs"   @ $16.95 =_____

"In the Shadow of the Rockies"   @ $16.95 =_____

"Dynamite Hill"   @ $16.95 =_____

Shipping and handling per book @ $ 5.00 =_____

                                7% GST =_____

Total amount enclosed: _____

Make cheque or money order payable to:
Megamy Publishing Ltd.
Price subject to change without prior notice.
ORDERS OUTSIDE OF CANADA must be paid in U.S. funds by
cheque or money order drawn on U.S. or Canadian Bank.
Sorry no C.O.D.'s.